I0504827

Successful

Real Estate Selling

Successful

Real Estate Selling

How to Make Big Money
Even in Bad Markets

Thomas Mourning

iUniverse, Inc.

New York Lincoln Shanghai

Successful Real Estate Selling
How to Make Big Money Even in Bad Markets

Copyright © 2007 by Thomas N. Mourning

All rights reserved. No part of this book may be used or reproduced by any means, graphic, electronic, or mechanical, including photocopying, recording, taping or by any information storage retrieval system without the written permission of the publisher except in the case of brief quotations embodied in critical articles and reviews.

iUniverse books may be ordered through booksellers or by contacting:

iUniverse
2021 Pine Lake Road, Suite 100
Lincoln, NE 68512
www.iuniverse.com
1-800-Authors (1-800-288-4677)

The information, ideas, and suggestions in this book are not intended to render professional advice. Before following any suggestions contained in this book, you should consult your personal accountant or other financial advisor. Neither the author nor the publisher shall be liable or responsible for any loss or damage allegedly arising as a consequence of your use or application of any information or suggestions in this book.

ISBN-13: 978-0-595-41457-4 (pbk)
ISBN-13: 978-0-595-85806-4 (ebk)
ISBN-10: 0-595-41457-5 (pbk)
ISBN-10: 0-595-85806-6 (ebk)

Printed in the United States of America

Contents

INTRODUCTION

Why This Book Will Help You Make More Money Selling Real Estate

This simple, no-nonsense, practical, proven information has worked for me and many others. This is not theory. This is not double-talk.

The recommendations I make in this book will help you maximize your effectiveness in earning more with the limited time and energy you have available.

While this book focuses primarily on how to make more money selling real estate, you can also learn to sell anything else using this information. Tangibles. Intangibles. Automobiles. Insurance. Boats. Advertising. You name it. I have personally used these techniques to set sales records in other fields. You can do the same.

I have spent over twenty years in the field of real estate setting sales record after sales record, enjoying accolades and the fruits of the commission income I received.

In addition, I have developed some of the most profitable offices in the country. After working with real estate agents and others in my training, I feel comfortable telling you that these simple, clear, how-to directions work. The instructions are all here for you to use, starting today. Professionally mastered audiotapes of this material are also available. For more information, check my Web site at TomMourning.com.

Learn What Mistakes to Avoid

In this book, you'll learn exactly what mistakes to avoid, even if you're a beginner. You can bank on this because I remember my own problems as a beginner as vividly as if they were happening today.

There was so much I wanted and needed to know to get listings and sales instead of turndowns, put-offs, or buyer's remorse. There is nothing as expensive as a blown sale.

After analyzing hundreds of my own personal sales and listings—and those of agents working for me—I learned what I did wrong. I'm sharing that information so you can learn from my mistakes.

Your new know-how will guide you to make relatively simple, swift changes that will lead to more listings and sales. The same simple facts of selling keep working for me. The many successful agents whom I've taught and guided through the years prove the effectiveness of these sales secrets.

I'm revealing my sales secrets to you because we real estate agents are interdependent. Most of your transactions will be with another agent. Wouldn't it be better for the industry—and for each of us—if everyone we worked with was a pro? I have taught brand-new agents to become top producers. I have taught top producers to double and triple their incomes.

I'm proud of them all, as I will be of you when I hear how you have used these tips to increase your income.

Increase Your Sales Earnings

If you are in another sales field, this practical information will help you make more money for your efforts. If you are thinking about getting into the real estate field, this information should help you decide. It should also give you the enthusiasm and confidence to be a top producer, a superstar. If you are new to real estate, this information will give you the tools to tremendously accelerate your learning curve.

You won't have to reinvent the wheel. You won't make those costly mistakes. You won't accept the results of the average agent. You can be making a superstar income immediately.

If you have been in real estate for some time and are producing only average earnings, you can use this information to change that sad fact overnight. If you are already a top producer, you can use this information to double your production, or you may use the information to produce the same results in half the time.

To help you better understand this information, I use many personal, real-life examples. In doing so, I'm not trying to blow my own horn, but to provide you with the how-to specifics I've learned in my years of award-winning real estate sales and management.

Compact, easy-to-digest paragraphs provide answers to questions I've received from beginning, intermediate, and superstar agents in real-life situations and during courses, seminars, and sales meetings I've led.

Use the Scripts

Use my scripts, word for word. Do not deviate.

Pretend you are an actor. You are on stage. If you blow your lines, you're out of work. You blow your lines, and there's no food on the family's table.

You get it right, and forget the family's table; we're talking Paris for lunch!

Work toward Results. Do Not Dream Empty Dreams

From now on, you must set your course, guided by the precepts here and your talent and dreams. Realize that, from this step forward, by using this proven information, you will actually be moving toward your goals. You won't be just fumbling, dreaming, or yearning to be a success.

I believe it is a noble aim to help people in what is probably the most important financial transaction in their lives. In this book, my goal is to help you to live your happiest, most productive, most rewarding life, helping people maximize the results of those important financial transactions.

I recommend that you refer to this book repeatedly. Some of my agents actually keep my materials on their car seats to refer to just before going in on a listing appointment. I also find myself referring to the materials regularly. We all need reminders.

Use All the Information

To become a top-producing sales agent with the income that comes with that, I urge you to read and use all of the information in this book, from cover to cover. If you don't, you won't gain maximum benefit. I've had agents tell me that they prefer to do listing presentations my way and work with buyers in another way, only to later find to their chagrin and expense that they lost a buyer they shouldn't have or worked with a looker—someone who is just looking—too long.

As you proceed, use a pencil to check those pointers you want to remember. Reread them repeatedly in the future to build deep-seated confidence and expertise. Each chapter will help you get accepted contracts. These chapters will tell you what to do, and what not to do, to get that listing signed at the right price with a full commission; to get that buyer's offer signed today; and to get that seller's acceptance signed right now without getting put off or rejected.

Of course, you must apply the time and effort necessary to reap the rewards. Planning and talking are all part of it. But that's not selling. Ultimately, selling means finding motivated buyers and sellers and making something happen. To do that, you must find them, get out among them, ask the right questions, discover their needs, handle their objections, get their signatures on a contract, follow up, get the transaction closed, and have happy referral-giving clients or even an entire cheering section on your hands.

Let's get to work.

CHAPTER ONE

To Succeed at Selling, Do Not Reinvent the Wheel

I decided to write this book when a fellow manager asked me, "How in the world do you break all those sales records and develop those top offices?"

I'm glad he asked. I had never really thought about what I did to achieve that kind of success. In a nutshell, what I had figured out was there was nothing new in real estate.

There have always been superstar producers in this field, and they've all pretty much done the same things.

I'm not saying it's simple. Obviously, it's not. If it were, everybody would be a real estate superstar. I'm saying that there is a common denominator in all top producers' activities.

The bottom line is: For you to be successful, you must do the things successful people do. Conversely, you must not do the things average agents (from here we'll call average agents, AA's) do.

Average agents always try to reinvent the wheel.

Once I figured this out, I made it a point to learn everything I could from successful agents. I took them to lunch, asked questions, and listened. It was amazing. Then I did what those successful agents told me to do, and it worked for me, too.

I also made it a point to talk to AA's. I concluded that if you figure out what the AA's do, and do just the opposite, that will work for you, too.

To Succeed, Do Not Do What Average Agents Do

AA's do not talk to lots of people. In addition, when AA's do talk to someone, they only talk. They don't ask questions and listen to the answers.

AA's are needy. They seek approval by giving away information like addresses on ad calls, by showing without probing, by accepting put-offs, and by a willingness to work with a buyer for six months. When asked why, the AA says, "It's the only buyer I've got."

The AA is just "trying real estate" and has no long-term commitment. He does not follow up. He does not educate his clients and make them part of the loop. Rather, he lets them dictate prices, commissions, and even appointment times. He closes three or four transactions a year and thinks real estate is a "lousy business."

Of course, it is—for him.

The AA's focus is on the commission, not on the subsequent referral. To get clients, he relies on office advertising during his floor time. When agents in the office are assigned times to handle incoming inquiries from sign and ad calls, it's called floor time. The AA blows most of the calls he gets. He hardly ever holds open houses. When he does, he watches the game on TV and ignores his prospects. He never sees For Sale by Owners (FSBOs) or expired listings. (An expired is what we call a seller whose listing has been on the market and didn't sell during the term of the listing, a negotiable period, but usually ninety days. A listing is a contract between the sellers and the broker that specifies the price, the term, and the commission.) He doesn't like to talk to his friends about real estate. When he does, it's with little or no enthusiasm; or worse, he's negative. In addition, he never follows up a conversation about real estate by asking for a referral. He shows up at the office late, leaves early, and considers himself overworked. He thinks that successful people in real estate are lucky.

If you think this is cynical, you're right. It's gloomy, negative, and derisive. It's also pretty accurate. If you don't believe me, check with the National Association of Realtors. That organization found that over 65 percent of clients would not work with the same agent again. What was the main complaint? The clients never heard back from the agent. The client is under the impression that the agent just took the commission and ran. The client is right. Just ask someone with an expired listing. He'll give you an earful. The agent came over, took the listing, and the seller never heard from the agent again. It's criminal, it's stupid, and it's also very instructive. Don't do what the AA does.

If you ever need a reason to get out of bed in the morning to go to work, think of the AA. It will give you evangelistic fervor to think of your prospective client stuck with an average agent for the most important financial transaction in their lives. And he's your competition!

Superstars aren't your competition. They are your allies in your war against the real competition: the average agent. The superstar is easy to work with and is often fun. He makes things happen. He carries his load, unlike the AA for whom you'll wind up taking over the whole transaction. That's okay, though. Guess who'll get the referral from the AA's client?

If your competition is the AA, what are your chances for success in real estate sales?

To Succeed, Do What Successful Agents Do

I took the superstar agents to lunch, asked questions, shut up, and listened. I did the things these agents said to do, and these things worked for me, too. What did I find out? That's what this book is all about.

What does the successful agent look like? There are no common denominators in age, sex, looks, education, or background. Man or woman, fat or thin, black or white, tall or short, neat or sloppy, PhD or high-school dropout—so far, everybody qualifies.

We know the real estate business is not for everybody. And yet the fact remains that some people are extremely successful in real estate. So what makes the successful agent special?

The common denominators in successful real estate salespeople are the same denominators that you will find in successful people in every field: such successful people demonstrate commitment and perseverance. They have focus and discipline. They are enthusiastic, confident, and busy. They have high expectations for themselves and others. They specialize. They know their inventory. They know pricing (local real estate values) or how to price (how to determine valuation) if they don't. If one of these people says that a property is a good deal, it *is* a good deal. In addition, interestingly, as a rule, although they think highly of what they do, they don't think overly highly of themselves.

Successful real estate agents think it's easy. Let me say that again—they think it's easy. They are actually a little embarrassed about how much money they make with what they perceive as so little effort.

The interesting thing about all of these traits is that anyone can have them. Few do, but anyone can. Simply knowing about them will help you gain them.

I remember thinking after a particularly staggering closing month, "How could this be legal? I made more this month than I ever dreamed of making in a year. I've had fun. I've done whatever I've wanted to do. And, I'm not only having fun, I've got my own fan club of happy clients!"

The real estate business has been good to me. Maybe like the superstars, I'm a little embarrassed at how easy it was. Maybe greatness is easy. If someone had asked Mozart, Hemingway, Elvis, or even William Gates III that question, I have an idea that these successful people said, "Yep, nothing to it!"

So, for what it's worth, and not for one minute thinking I'm Mozart, Hemingway, or Elvis, I'll pass the information in this book along for you to use as you choose.

Basic Keys of Success

The authoritative book on success is Napoleon Hill's *Think, and Grow Rich*. It was written in the thirties and is, quite simply, the finest book ever written on the subject. I recommend multiple readings of it. You can probably find it at your library.

From years of researching the most successful men of his day, Hill concludes that there are three keys to success: specialized knowledge, burning desire, and persistence.

Key #1: Specialize

Specialized knowledge, for real estate agents, involves knowing what to do, what to say, and why. You also need to know the inventory and the technical aspects of real estate law, appraisal, and practice.

Many average agents have a good knowledge of the market and know how to fill out a contract, make disclosures, and price a property. A superstar, on the other hand, knows what the client is thinking, what the client might say and do, and knows exactly what to say and do in response to each of the client's concerns or situations.

Doesn't it make sense that if you know exactly what your client is going to say and do in a given situation, you can prepare a proactive response and be more effective?

Specializing, to the superstar, also means concentrating on one market. I know of one top agent who won't list or sell outside his neighborhood of 485 homes. He knows the power of specialization.

If you come across a client whose needs are not in your area of specialization, refer that individual to someone else. We'll talk about this when we get to the Rules. Specialization means focusing on a geographic location and kinds of real estate. If you want to be a superstar selling houses, don't try to sell ranches, apartment buildings, commercial property, industrial property, or business opportunities. Refer this business out to someone who specializes in those properties. Stay focused on your specialty, and you will save yourself time, energy, and aggravation. You'll also be much more likely to get paid.

Key #2: Ya Gotta Wanna!

Burning desire is a major "wanna." It's not "want to." You can "want" lots of things and never get them. Burning desire is feeling so strongly for a cause that you're willing to die for it. That's "wanna."

Read the book *The Five Rings*. It's the story of an ancient warrior who retired in his sixties to live in a cave in self-disgrace. He chose to do so because in over six hundred major battles, he didn't die for his master. To him, death was the ultimate success. That's "wanna."

I've seen agents pin a picture of a high-priced automobile in front of them at their desk. They keep thinking about getting that car. It consumes them. One fine day, they come walking into my office with big grins and ask, "Like to see my new car?"

That's "wanna" at work.

Have you ever heard someone say, "My kids are going to have it better than me?"

You know he means it by that look in his eye. That's "wanna." That's burning desire.

Planning and goal setting develop burning desire. So plan big. Big plans stir the emotions and get you excited. In fact, you'll get so excited you won't want to wait to get started. Can you make plans big enough in real estate sales to stir your soul?

Think about this. Real estate superstars do two hundred transactions a year. Since housing prices vary so much from decade to decade and region to region, the amount of the transactions in dollar volume doesn't count. Numbers of closed transactions in unit volume are what count for this discussion. Two hundred deals. If you figure out how superstars did two hundred deals, and you realize they're mere mortals just like you, do you think you could do fifty deals? What would fifty deals mean to you in commission income in your market? It's only one deal a week. Think about it.

Key #3: Persist!

Persistence is simply the tenacity required to do whatever is necessary to achieve your goal. Why is it that the greatest success often comes after some major failure? Why is it that for most people the mother lode is just inches away when they quit? I don't know. That's just how it is.

One of my teachers once told my class that this fellow David Hume says that if something happens five times in a row, it's likely not to happen the next time. I remarked that if I were to stand in front of a train going a hundred miles an hour and it hurt me all five times, chances are real good I'd avoid standing in front of trains in the future. The teacher rubbed his chin, thought about it, and said I was brilliant. He'd never really thought about it that way. The mysteries of academia. Don't fight the system.

Failure happens. Ask a billionaire, "Did you ever fail?"

He'll look at you like you're nuts. Of course he's failed. He'd probably tell you that he succeeded more than others did because he failed more than others did. Since he's the billionaire, maybe you should take his word for it.

It's one of life's great paradoxes. In the movie *Patton*, General Patton says, "How can there be heroes without cowards?"

How can there be peace without war? How can there be life without death? How can there be success without failure? So go out and fail. Count on it. Plan on it. Besides, what's the fun in winning every time?

The major purpose of this book is to teach you specialized knowledge, proven successful techniques, and scripts to maximize your prospecting and presentation efforts. These techniques and scripts work. They will give you the confidence you need. In addition, you'll find planning and goal-setting techniques to fuel your burning desire for success.

It is critical to see the relationship between specialized knowledge and attitude. The knowledge and ability you will gain by reading this book are only 33 percent of the total mix. The 67 percent balance is attitude: burning desire and persistence.

I can give you the specialized knowledge. It's up to you to learn it and use it. It's up to you to develop the attitude necessary for success. I can lead. I can point the way. I can show you models. I can't do it for you. You shouldn't let me if I could. That would take all the fun out of it.

Key #4: Believe, Sister and Brother!

Believe me when I tell you this information works. It has worked for me and many others. What's the worst thing that can happen if you believe it and somehow you find out it doesn't work? Well, you've probably tried dumber things. I sure have.

What's the best thing that can happen? You can become a real estate superstar and do the most fantastic things you can imagine with the money you earn. Take your friends to Paris for lunch. Make some shrewd investments along the way, and have a lot of fun in the meantime. Maybe you'll even write a book about your success.

The tips I've included here work. To be honest, I have had people come to me and say, "I tried it. It doesn't work."

However, when I asked these people to repeat what they tried to me, it was not exactly like I said to do it. We'd go over it again a couple of times, and I'd send them off to try again.

After such a refresher course from me, one of these fellows then went out and got ten out of eleven listing presentations in just one month. Those listings all sold and closed.

One fellow went out and got thirty-six straight listings. He had better be careful, or he may have to hire a major accounting firm to handle all of his income.

I encourage you to believe, but also to question. That's the best way to learn. Why? What? How come? How does that apply to me? Imagine yourself in the situation. How would that work for you?

Repeat it. It takes many repetitions before it becomes a part of you. Repeat it and drill.

Practice scripts on your friends, your spouse, or a buddy at the office. Drill until your responses become automatic. If your client says, "You guys still at 6 percent?"

Bang. You have four responses that you know will work, right on the tip of your tongue. The client says, "I'll think about it."

Boom. You know exactly how he feels. After all, it's a big decision, isn't it? You know just what to say and do about it.

The client says, "Does the refrigerator come with the house?"

Wham. You know all the subtext to that one, and you know just the response that's most effective every time.

The client asks, "Why don't we price the house at [some ridiculous price] and see what happens?"

Zing. You don't get mad. You don't argue. You educate. You make him part of the loop, an insider.

I've devoted a whole chapter for you on that one. You'll know it cold. You'll be so excited when he says it. Can you imagine? Excited to get an objection? You won't be able to wait to try out all this great stuff and watch it work!

Excited? Can you be excited just because you know some stuff that works in situations that you know will come up, and come up all the time? You bet. Dreams are made of the stuff. The AA gets one out of four listing presentations.

With these techniques, with this specialized knowledge, you will get three out of four. Guess what else? You are going to go out on a lot more listing presentations.

Key #5: You Gotta Get Past the Fo Dogs

So, you read, reread, practice, and drill, drill, drill. Is it possible to know this material perfectly, have a plan, burning desire, and persistence, and still fail? It's difficult, but possible. How?

"The only way into the temple is past the Fo Dogs of Fear and Greed," says a Buddhist philosophy (Fo Dogs are also known as Chinese Lions of Buddha). I'm sure you've seen the two lions (dogs, it turns out) outside doors in Chinatown. That's what they signify. That's what can cause you to fail. Fear on one side and greed on the other. To get into the temple, to attain success, you gotta get past them.

Look at the AA. He's broke and down on his luck. When he does a deal, he counts the commission before he gets it. He sees the transaction as a commission instead of a potential referral source. This is greed. And it's not smart. Clients can smell greed a mile away. Do you think a client will pass a referral along to an agent they perceive as greedy? Can you imagine a fan club for a greedy real estate agent?

The AA is also afraid—afraid to try; afraid of rejection; afraid of failure; afraid to be unsophisticated; afraid to *succeed*. Bouncing off fear and greed, you can rest assured that the AA will never make it into the temple.

The average buyer and seller also operate from fear and greed. After all, a house is the biggest investment most people ever make in their lifetime. Knowing that buyers and sellers experience fear and greed allows us to use this knowledge to educate them in pricing and negotiating.

Key #6: Think Referrals, Not Commissions

Always remember that real estate is a long-term, referral-driven business. One of the nice things about this business is you never have to retire. You can be successful in real estate at age one hundred. Once you're on a roll, why not? There is simply nothing like being on a roll in real estate. I call it, "The upward ascending spiral."

Sometimes, nothing happens. You do your thing, and nothing happens. But in real estate, you keep trying and eventually, success happens. It will never be what you planned, mind you. You're working on a deal, and it falls through.

However, something else shows up that you never would have imagined, directly as a result of your efforts and contacts of that failed deal.

A superstar agent who likes to work maybe three months a year and makes more in that three months than four or five average agents do in a year said, "It's like taking a bicycle through the gears. It's tough working through the first gear, but when you get to third gear, it seems so easy!"

Another nice thing about the real estate business: your time is your own. Take all of the time off you want. Hey, you're one hundred years old with this fantastic fan club of rabid supporters shoving referrals at you. Give the referrals to some young whippersnapper to do all the legwork. You make a few phone calls to make sure everybody's happy, and split the commission with him.

Never, ever, think about the commission. Sure, you're happy to take it when it comes. But what you really care about is the customer. Period. You have to be prepared to walk away from that commission in the blink of an eye. However, you're never prepared to walk away from your client's best interests.

Key #7: Quit Talking. Start Asking. And Listen!

Superstars don't talk. They ask questions and listen to the answers. Someone told me there's a book out, *Quit Selling!* What a fantastic title. Average agents think they are selling. They aren't. Please, quit selling.

One of the greatest seminars about selling I ever attended was put on by one of the world's greatest salesmen, a man named Al Tomsic. He said, "Selling is not telling. Selling is asking questions!"

The average agent tells. He talks too much.

Selling is not adversarial. Selling is harmony. How can you sell somebody when you don't know what he wants? Selling is agreement. How can you get agreement with your mouth flapping? I would venture to guess that more sales are lost from over-talking and selling than for any other single reason.

Tomsic also said this about handling objections, "Smile and agree, call them by name, and ask a question."

Try it at home sometime. The next time an argument comes up, after a warm smile say, "I can certainly understand that, honey. After all, it's just a fender. You know, Rolls Royces are tough to handle in a crowded supermarket parking lot. Do you think we should hire a driver?"

In negotiating, the first one to talk, loses. Ask questions, shut up, and listen. Never argue. Never get mad. Try to understand. Try to see if you can repeat the client's concern or objection, "I hear you saying that you don't like the size of the dining room. Is that true?"

Try to isolate the concern or objection. Ask, "Other than the size of the dining room, is there any other concern with this property?"

Try understanding, and try a question. "Well, I can certainly understand that. After all, this is a $200,000 home. It would be a shame to have to replace your dining room furniture. About how much do you think you could get for that dining room set in today's market? About how much would it cost to get one that fit? Do you suppose the seller would consider crediting that difference in your offer? Do you like the seller's dining room set? Do you suppose he would consider throwing it in with your offer? After all, you are exceptionally good buyers, aren't you?"

Come up with some creative solutions and watch what happens.

Here's what the buyer might say in response, "You know what, honey? I love this house. I've always hated Aunt Martha's dining room set. Here's the opportunity we've always looked for. Let's buy this house so we can dump Aunt Martha's dining room set."

Whatever works. The point is there is no way to talk them out of the fact that the dining room won't work for them. Find out why and come up with solutions.

Key #8: Act Like a Superstar

If you want to be a superstar, act like a superstar. What does a superstar look like? How does he or she dress? Act? Where does she live? What kind of car does he drive? What does she do? Don't know? Take one to lunch and ask. It's called, "Fake it until you make it!"

The subconscious is an amazing thing. You tell it you are a superstar. It goes right along with you. If you are not already a superstar but you think and act like one, chances are very good you'll become one. Ask yourself, "Is this the way my superstar would do it? Would my superstar waste any more time with these prospects? Is this how a superstar prepares for a listing presentation?"

Key #9: You Are Busy
You Know One Thing for Sure: Superstars Are Busy. So Get Busy.

Let your clients know, politely, of course, that you are busy. An agent walked into my office one day. She said that her new listing had just sold. She wanted me to know why it sold for almost full price in just two weeks.

She said that she met these clients who said they wanted to move up. She showed them property and wrote an offer, but it didn't work out because the people had a home to sell. These clients asked her to take the listing.

When she put on her presentation, they insisted on an unrealistic price, no sign, and no lockbox. She explained that under those circumstances, she would have to decline the listing. She excused herself and left.

Some months later, these clients called her back. It seemed they had finally purchased another house in another area and wanted to put their house on the market. She remembered their previous appointment and explained that she wouldn't be interested if they still had those same requirements.

She explained that she would be happy to assist them, but only if they didn't "tie her hands" in marketing the property. They agreed.

She went out, put on her presentation again, and this time told them, "This is what we're gonna do!"

They did it. And she did it.

She said, "I just wanted you to know, Tom, that you have taught us this until you were blue in the face. I finally took it in. I'm busy."

And a prospect for superstardom.

Key #10: Have Fun!

Don't take it all so seriously. This can be one of the greatest experiences in a buyer or seller's life. Or it can be one of the worst.

Humor helps. Life's too short. If it ain't fun, don't do it.

Makes sense to me!

CHAPTER TWO

Do You Really Want to Be a Salesperson?

The real estate business is a sales business. We get paid commissions. If we don't close the escrow, we don't get paid. We don't get paid for going to the office, previewing and showing property, going to seminars, taking listings, writing contracts, or finding and educating clients. In fact, it costs us time, energy, and money to do those things with absolutely no assurance we'll ever even be reimbursed.

Since it's a sales business, and we're investing our time, energy, and dollars, it seems reasonable that this is a process that deserves some serious thinking.

What is the sales business all about?

First, we all understand and agree that everybody's in the sales business. Billy's selling salvation. Willy's selling tax increases. Luigi's selling software. Momma is selling her little boy on the benefits of being good.

Everybody's trying to sell us something. Madison Avenue, the national media, and the factories all across the country would be out of work without it.

Let's face it; you are already in the sales business. Now, how do you want to get paid? Under what working conditions?

Is Commission Sales for You?

We're talking about commission sales. Straight commission sales means, of course, you can make as much or as little as you choose, depending upon your results. Nobody in commission sales has a boss who will give you a pay raise for showing up for work on time, keeping a neat desk, and being pleasant to your customers and fellow workers.

The downsides to the real estate business are inconsistent income, irregular hours, and weekend work. The upsides of the real estate business are inconsistent income, irregular hours, and weekend work. Why would I take the advantages over the disadvantages? Why, for example, if I could make $50,000 a year consistently for just showing up from nine to five, Monday through Friday, would I risk the inconsistency and irregularity of a commission income?

Why? Because I could make $20,000 inconsistently a month, working six days a week with Thursdays off. Or maybe $10,000 a month, working four days a week with three months of vacation and no boss. Sound crazy? Believe me; these numbers are very, very conservative. There are agents out there making over $100,000 a month. I know this because I was one of them. I didn't make that much every month. Isn't an inconsistent $100,000 a month better than that consistent income you have now?

When you start talking about those kinds of dollars, the inconsistency and the hours begin to pale in their importance. I mean, if you can make more in a month than you make in a whole year, you could probably figure out a way to budget irregularity in your income, couldn't you?

Besides, who's to say the $50,000-a-year salary really is consistent? Because of mergers, acquisitions, and a depressed economy, thousands upon thousands of people have been laid off. Twenty some years ago, I had a good job with a major corporation. I was making $1,500 a month with a company car and an expense account, a nice wife, three little kids, and a house in the suburbs. I had it made, right? I caught the 6:30 AM bus into the city to go to work. I got home at 6:30 PM, taking the last bus out. I worked nearly every weekend, just keeping up on the paperwork. I spent more than I was earning, and I was young and ambitious. I would have cut off my arm to make $30,000 a year. At that time, young guys didn't make $30,000 a year. I had a big job as it was.

One day, my boss brought me in and gave me a review that was terrible. I couldn't believe my ears. My life passed in front of my eyes. He didn't fire me. He just laid me out real good. I thought about it. I started going to night school, and I got my real estate license. I started doing real estate part-time.

My first weekend, I was in the office, and an agent called for someone to cover for him at his open house so he could get some lunch. I agreed.

Another agent from another company was showing the property to a couple, and they were just sitting down to write up an offer. I excused myself and went out front. A couple drove up and asked me questions. I answered them and explained that someone else was now in the house, writing an offer. The couple got excited thinking that maybe this might be the very house for them and somebody else was making an offer on it.

They asked, "Can we see it?"

I replied, "Oh, I guess it would be all right as long as we don't disturb the buyers."

You guessed it. They bought it. It was my first day in the business, and they bought it. I thought, "This is sure an easy business!" I soon quit my big corporation job.

That first year in the business, I made $63,000. House prices were a tenth of today's prices. I paid off all my bills and paid cash for a new Mercedes. Incredible. That's commission sales. That's what inconsistent income can do for you.

Just a few years later, that big corporation I worked for was acquired by a big investor, chopped up, and sold off in pieces. The investor made a billion dollars. All the employees lost their jobs—everybody, even my old boss. That's what a consistent income will do for you.

Okay. You agree that this commission sales business is one fantastic opportunity. Maybe you are already in the business and starving. Maybe you are already in the business and love it, but want to do more. How?

How did I do it? How did all those superstars I took to lunch say to do it? Good question. First, let me ask you some questions.

Pop Quiz

Question: What is your single, most important job as a real estate agent? What exactly is the most critical thing you must do in order to earn a commission?

Pick only one from below:

1. Close escrows.

2. Educate clients.

3. Find motivated clients.

4. Fire unmotivated clients.

5. Follow up.

6. Go on listing appointments.

7. Present offers.

8. Show property.

9. Write contracts.

Which answer did you pick? _____

Why?

What do you believe are the next eight things you should do, in order of importance?

2.

3.

4.

5.

6.

7.

8.

Why?

Define motivated:

Explain the difference between high-impact and low-impact prospecting:

Rank the following prospecting methods in order of effectiveness and efficiency in finding motivated clients:

___Cold door knocking

___Cold phone calling

___Calling on expireds

___Farming

___Floor time

___Calling on FSBOs

___Open house

___Warm calls

Why?

How can this information be helpful to you in your business planning and goal setting?

You'll find the answers to the quiz in the next chapter. Please don't go on until you've answered the questions to the best of your ability. Keep these questions in mind as you proceed.

CHAPTER THREE

Prospecting for the Motivated Client

Let's think about the questions on that Pop Quiz you just took. You are in commission sales. You don't get paid until an escrow closes. Let's start with that.

The first thing you need to do is close an escrow. The answer is number one, right? Well, you can't close an escrow until you open one. In order to open one, you need to get a contract signed, either from a buyer to whom you've shown property or a seller whose listing you have taken.

So, the answer is number nine, "Write contracts." Right? Well, you can't write contracts unless you've shown property, qualified buyers, or gone on a listing appointment. In addition, you can't even do any of that until you've found a client.

And, even then, you can't write a contract that will close escrow unless the client is motivated.

That's right. The answer is number three.

Major Concept #1: Your Number One Job Is Finding Motivated Clients

Clearly, nothing happens in the commission sales business until you have found a client who is motivated enough to sign a market-value contract. I know you'll find this difficult to believe, as this concept seems so simple, so elemental, so basic and logical, but most real estate agents simply don't get it. If they got it, they all would have more clients than they could handle. They would be forced to refer out a sizable number of their buyers and sellers. I can assure you that this is not the case with agents, except, of course, the superstars.

What a superstar does is prospect. Prospecting, of course, in the sales business, means looking for clients like the old forty-niners looked for gold. They were called prospectors. Superstars have found the mother lode.

The superstar prospects to the exclusion of anything else until he or she finds enough clients to meet their plan. There are lots of very productive methods of prospecting. We'll go into detail about the ones that worked best for me. All of them seem to work. Problem is, you must do it. It will not come to you.

The AA thinks it will. He's dead wrong. He goes to the office and works on his files, has a cup of coffee, goes on tour of listed properties with a buddy in the office, holds an occasional open house, takes his floor time, and makes an occasional phone call to the few clients he has. I'm not kidding. That's his day. Do you see something missing here? This is a guaranteed unmitigated disaster in the making.

As a commission-earning salesperson, your most important job, to the exclusion of everything else until it's done, is prospecting. Prospecting for what? Clients, right? Okay, but what kind of clients? Motivated clients.

Major Concept #2: "Motivated" Means "Has To"

What Concept #1 means is that my job is looking for buyers and sellers.

Concept #2 says that the person most likely to buy or sell is one that *has to* buy or sell. Therefore, the people I'm looking for in my prospecting are those who *have to*. Who are these people? Transferees. People in the midst of divorces. Bank foreclosures. Builders.

That doesn't mean that I won't work with others, primarily renters, move-ups, and move-downs. It simply means that, given a choice, I'd rather work with someone who *has to sell or buy*. Practically speaking, since I'm very busy, I'll give others a little of my time, but I'll leave them in a heartbeat if I think they are wasting it and can't make a decision.

A lot of people *have to* buy or sell. They need your expertise. An unmotivated buyer tends to make lowball offers. An unmotivated seller will tend to insist on pricing their property over market value. Sorry. I haven't got time for that.

Look at it this way. Let's say your plan is to make $120,000 in the next year. That's $10,000 a month, $2,500 a week, and $62.50 an hour.

Some unmotivated client thinks he wants to buy a house. You spend four hours putting together homes to see, making appointments, driving to the properties, qualifying the buyers, and touring the properties. You show them the absolute best values for their needs and finances on the market. There is nothing better out there now and probably there never will be. You know the market, cold.

The client doesn't buy one of the houses. You didn't sell your way out of the sale. He just won't write a contract. If he did, it would be for a low price.

What just happened? Somebody just stole $250 from you. That's what happened. Four hours of your time is worth $250. He just took it from you and forgot to pay.

After all, you agreed to do the work on the come, for the prospect of a commission. You can't bill them. However, you can do something. What would you do if somebody was working for you and stole $250 out of your petty cash? Right. You fire them.

What you do is refer them out to another agent. Superstars have so many clients that they have to refer some of them anyway. You do that. I have done it many times in my career. I have never been paid a referral fee on one of those referred clients. Maybe the agent forgot my referral fee. I doubt it.

Since we are being picky here, and since this is our book, is there any other attribute other than motivated that we'd like to see in our prospect? Well, now that you mention it, there is.

Major Concept #3: The Best Client Is the Motivated Personal Referral

Let's face it. The best client would probably be your mom. However, she can buy only so many houses. It's the same with your friends and relatives. If the clients are referred by someone you know, wouldn't that be almost as good? Sure. Wouldn't it be easier to work with someone to whom you were recommended than to work with someone you didn't know? Of course. It's easier and a lot more fun.

Fifty percent of solving a problem is identifying the problem. We just identified our problem. Our number one job is to find a motivated personal referral.

Okay, we're halfway home. We've identified our problem. Now, how do we solve it? How do we find these folks? Should we ask the average agent? What does he think? He thinks that after he's in the business long enough, clients will come to him. How's that for a clue? Guess what? Right! It doesn't work that way.

You gotta ask for the referral.

One day while holding an open house, an agent and his client walked in and soon started to write a contract. In the normal course of conversation with the client, I found out he was being transferred into town by a well-known local company. I didn't show my feelings to the agent and the client, but I got very upset. Why didn't my brother-in-law give me this referral?

This client worked for the same company as my brother-in-law, who I saw three or four nights a week. To whom, by the way, I had just loaned some money. Oh, was I hot. I called him. I asked if he knew this client. He said that the guy was moving in to the office next to his. I could barely contain myself. This is how I fed his wife's nieces and nephew.

He said, "Wait a minute, Tom. It's not my job to worry about your business. I got enough to worry about with my own. It's not my job. It's your job. It's your job to ask me."

You know what? He was right. That totally changed my perspective on prospecting. It also made me a lot of money, saved me a lot of time, and made my job substantially easier and more fun.

You gotta ask. It's okay. People expect it. After all, *it is your job*.

Major Concept #4: The Most Efficient Way to Get Motivated Personal Referrals Is with WDYK

Okay, so you gotta ask. Who do you ask? What's the best way to ask?
Glad you asked. WDYK. You ask, "Who Do You Know?"

CHAPTER FOUR

WDYK?

We have now figured out how you can make more money in commissions selling real estate. You must find motivated personal referral clients.

Spending the limited time and energy you have available with motivated personal referral clients will give you the most bang for your buck. I hope my logic here is clear. It's far better to spend your time looking for motivated people than it is working with people who *think* they want to buy or sell.

Searching for the Motivated Personal Referral

Let me say it another way. As an independent contractor, I'm free to work with anyone I choose. I am not required to spend my time with people who will not ultimately close an escrow.

This is how I earn my living. This is how I put food on my family's table. It is a business. As for me, I choose to make it a profitable and productive one. This is not the chamber of commerce. I am not a bush pilot, tour guide, babysitter, or taxicab driver. Esteemed professions all, I am sure.

My business is selling property. I'm good at it. Lots of people out there need my services. I cannot and will not waste my time with people who *think* they need my services. I will only work with those people who can *use* my services.

To the Exclusion of Everything Else

If I don't have anyone today who can *use* my services, I will spend my time, *to the exclusion of everything else*, to find those who do. I know people needing my services are out there. There are deals being made right now. Right now.

How come I'm not making those deals? Is an average agent out there botching one of those deals? If I'm not making a deal, and an average agent is botching it, it's my fault. It's my fault if I missed that deal because I was working with an unmotivated client.

When I say "to the exclusion of everything else," what do I mean? I don't eat or sleep? I ignore my current listings, escrows, and buyers? No. I mean that I will prospect today until I make an appointment with a motivated client. That might take five minutes or it might take five hours. Whatever the time commitment, you must do it.

Think about what this means. You want to get this out of the way as quickly as you possibly can. When you get this out of the way, you've done your job, and you can go home and have a life.

On the Pop Quiz, I asked if you knew the difference between high-impact and low-impact prospecting. There was a list of the most common forms of prospecting, which you were asked to rank in order of effectiveness.

Low-impact prospecting means prospecting in which you have no control and no way of determining in advance the potential results. Floor time is a perfect example.

Although floor time may work very well in your office, there is absolutely no way you can predict what will happen on any given day. It's the same with farming and with open houses. Not that these methods don't work. They do. The problem is that you can't be certain they will work right away, and you've got a commitment to get that appointment today.

Maximizing Prospecting Control and Predictability through High-Impact Prospecting

High-impact prospecting means prospecting where you have control and can reasonably predict, in advance, the potential results. Cold doors and cold phones are a perfect example.

Cold doors mean going out into a neighborhood and knocking on doors of people you don't know to talk about real estate. Cold phones is the same thing, only done on the telephone. It works. Studies have shown that you will get at least one lead with every hundred calls.

I know an agent who hires a telemarketer to make three hundred calls a day. That agent goes on a listing appointment every night. Isn't that great? However, it seems like a lot of work to me. Could there be a simpler way?

Expireds and FSBOs are one in ten. I personally love FSBOs. We'll talk about them later.

WDYK, if done correctly, is one in three.

WDYK Means "Who Do You Know?"

WDYK is the most efficient, high-impact prospecting you can do, per Major Concept #4.

Remember, our goal, objective, and commitment is to make an appointment with a motivated personal referral client today. Not tomorrow. Not maybe. Today. For sure.

We can sit and hope someone calls as a result of our farm letters. We can wait for people to come to our open houses. We can kill time waiting around for calls on our floor time. Or we can take action and make things happen. Hoping and wishing and waiting won't solve the problem today. That's what I know for sure.

Seems logical to me that we want to make things happen as quickly and easily as possible. Low-impact forms of prospecting involve hoping and waiting. To make things happen, you must do high-impact prospecting.

High-impact prospecting includes cold phones and doors. Cold calls are proven to generate one lead out of a hundred. FSBOs and expireds are proven one in ten. Social calls or warm calls are about the same, unless you do them right. If you do them right, they can be one in three. In other words, you make three phone calls to people you know, and if you do it correctly, you will, on average, get one lead.

Trying to simplify, I decided that if I had to make an appointment today, I'd do it in the easiest way I could. Why make one hundred phone calls if three would serve just as well?

Make and Work a "Living List"

The very first thing you should do is make a list of everybody you know. Your list should have at least 150 names on it. (If you don't have 150 names, do cold calls, asking people if they'd like to be on your mailing list. See #4, below.)

Keep the list with you at all times. You can add names as you think of new ones and as you meet new people.

Work the list. Sit down at your desk. Pick up the phone and call. Use the script word for word. As you call, do these other things:

1. Write a note on a card saying how nice it was talking to the people you call. Drop it in the mail. Today.

2. Make notes of any special events the individual may bring up in the conversation. Kid's birthdays. Anniversaries. Birthdays. Special ceremonies. Then calendar those things for a follow-up call and card.

3. Expunge the list. If there is anyone you call who makes you feel uncomfortable, take them off the list.

4. In the course of the conversation, mention that you have a little newsletter about trends in real estate that you put out about once a month. Ask if they'd like to be on the mailing list.

5. Of course, they're already on the list. Mail the newsletter monthly to everyone on your list. Then you can call and ask if they received the newsletter. It gives you a reason to follow up.

6. Send them a "Just Listed" or "Just Sold" card every time you list or sell something. You'd like to see them get something from you in the mail at least once a week.
Sound like a lot of work? It's still better than knocking on a hundred doors.

7. Find and highlight "Nosy Rosies," people who really enjoy knowing what everybody else is up to. They love being a resource. They excel at it, particularly with the money you are going to pay them. Put them at the top of your list. A good Nosy Rosie is good for four or five deals a year.

8. Pay them a finder's fee. Cash. The day it closes. Crisp, new one-hundred-dollar bills. Is this illegal? No. The California Department of Real Estate says that you can pay any fee you want for introduction to prospects as long as the person you pay doesn't do anything that would require a license. Giving you a name does not require a license. If you are in another state, check out the laws there.

How much money should you pay for referrals? It's up to you. Whatever will get you the referral. If I promised you ten crisp one-hundred-dollar bills if a deal closed, would you want to provide me with a referral that led to a ten-thousand-dollar commission?

The WDYK Script Works. Use It Word for Word.

Use the following WDYK script word for word. Do not deviate. Pretend you are an actor. You are on stage. You blow your lines; you're out of work. You blow your lines and there's no food on the family's table. You get it right, and forget the family table; we're talking Paris for lunch!

Remember, you are calling people you know who presumably like you and would be pleased to help you out if they could. They can. The National Association of Realtor's statistics show that the average person hears of someone moving three and a half times a year. In other words, like I said, about every third time you call.

Go to your desk. Pick up the phone. Punch in the number. Your friend answers the phone. Here's your script:

"Hi, (name of person). How are you doing?" (Pretty tough, so far, huh?)

"How are things?" (Ask about something you know the person is interested in) or, as a variation in subsequent calls:

"Did you get my newsletter?"

Wait.

Listen to the response. Be sincerely interested.

Eventually, what will the person ask you? Right. The person will ask you how real estate is going. Doesn't everybody always ask that when talking to a real estate person?

If the question doesn't come up, the person may not remember that you work in real estate. Simply find an appropriate moment and say, "By the way, did you know I'm in the real estate business?" That gives the individual a chance to say, "Really. How's it going?"

With a big smile (you do know that people can hear smiles on the phone, don't you?), and with enthusiasm, your scripted reply is:

"Fantastic! Business is incredible!"

Without pausing, say something upbeat about you and/or your office. The wording here is flexible, so you can say something current and truthful, but the rhythm and timing must be similar to

"Our office is breaking all kinds of sales records. We're selling everything we can get our hands on and more," or "I've had an incredible week. I've already sold two of my listings, and I've got a buyer coming in from Cincinnati tomorrow."

Do you get the feeling of the rhythm? Now, without pausing, say the following, word for word:

"In fact, my biggest problem in life right now is inventory. Who do you know that might be thinking of selling?"

Pause. *Do not talk*. Wait for a response. Listen carefully. Do not speak until the person answers.

Eventually, the person will answer. He will either say, "As a matter of fact ..." or give you a referral. Or, he will say, "Um ... Gee, I can't think of anybody."

If he says he can't think of anybody, immediately ask, "Anybody on your street?"
He says, "Um ... no."
You say, "Anybody at your office?"
He says, "Um ... no."
You say, "Anybody at your golf club?"
He says, "Um ... no."
You say, "Anybody at your church?"
He says, "Why, yes. As a matter of fact ..."

Bingo!

Sometimes people say, "Gee, I can't think of anybody that's thinking of selling, but I do know of someone thinking of buying."

That's okay, too!

Always ask four times, or until you get a referral. Advertising studies have shown that it sometimes takes four tries until the listener gets the message.

If you want to get one referral out of every three calls, you need to make sure your contacts get your message.

A Variation of the WDYK Script

One of the most successful superstars I have ever known used a variation of the WDYK script. She specialized in working with first-time buyers and investors in small, single-family homes.

She prided herself in knowing the inventory. She knew everything on the market and about to be on the market. She was always looking for the "good deal" properties she would talk up.

When she was out and about, at the beauty salon, or in line at the grocery store, she always let people know she was in real estate. She always had two or three deal properties.

People would always ask her how the real estate business was. She would reply with tremendous enthusiasm, "It's incredible. I've already sold three houses this week. But, I've just seen the most fantastic house."

She would go on to describe it in glowing superlatives. "I would love to sell that house to somebody. Who do you know that might be looking for a house like that?"

Do WDYK All the Time, Wherever You Go

Don't do WDYK only while you're on the phone or in a planned way. Do it with everyone. I went to a Chamber of Commerce luncheon with one of my agents. He sat next to me. Sitting on the other side of him was a local bank manager he did not personally know.

The bank manager politely asked the agent what he did for a living.

My agent looked at me in acknowledgment of being presented the script I had taught him, looked back at the bank manager, and replied, "I'm in the real estate business here."

The bank manager said, "Really. How's business?"

My agent, with a big grin, probably to show me how he was going to do my thing perfectly and let me watch it not work, said, "Fantastic! Business is booming. In fact our office is breaking all kinds of sales records."

Before he could go on, the bank manager interrupted and said, "You've got to be kidding. I heard that the real estate business is terrible."

My agent said, "Actually, I've got just the opposite problem. I just had ten escrows close last month." (This was true. And he did it using WDYK and the listing presentation you'll soon learn.)

"In fact, my biggest problem in life is inventory. Who do you know that's thinking of selling?"

The bank manager looked at him, flabbergasted, and said, "Well, as a matter of fact, my husband's best friend was just notified that he's been transferred."

My agent got out his notebook and took the referral. He sure showed me a thing or two, didn't he?

When You Get a Referral, Follow Up Immediately

You say, "WDYK?"

He says, "Well, as a matter of fact ..."

What do you do now? You do *whatever it takes* to get in contact with that referral immediately. Not next week. Not tomorrow. Not an hour from now. Now. Right now. Immediately.

I was brand new in real estate when I wrote a contract for a builder. Actually, I had car signs on the sides of my car, and I met him because he waved me down in my car. He wanted to see some lots my office had listed. He wanted to buy one. I wrote it up. I called the listing agent. She said to call the developer directly and present the offer, as the developer was a broker himself. I presented the offer. He signed it.

As we were talking afterward, I thought I'd do something nuts. Why not? When you're hot, you're hot. I told him I was brand new in the business and needed some inventory. Did he know anyone who was thinking of selling? He told me about his neighbor, who had been transferred to Denver. I asked if it would be all right if I called the neighbor. He had no problem with that, and I got the neighbor's phone number. I asked if it would be okay if I used his phone to make the call right now. He handed me his phone. I called. The man answered and asked me to come right on over.

I listed the house that day. At market price. Full commission. Sold in two weeks. As I was leaving, after getting the listing signed, the client told me I was a very lucky guy. I agreed and asked why he thought so. He said that when the phone rang with my call, he was just reaching for it to call another office to list his house.

He was right. I am a very lucky guy. How would you like to be lucky, too? Call instantly as soon as you get a referral.

One of my agents came into my office one day. "Got a WDYK referral yesterday," he said.

"Great!" said I.

"I called them last night for hours and, when I finally got through, they said they had just listed the house not an hour before."

"Bad luck," said I.

He said, "Maybe. I probably should have called as soon as I got the referral. But I was awfully busy."

Yes, sir. Too busy to make a phone call that would have made him $10,000. Now that's busy. Bad luck, too.

I know that sounds cynical. It is.

Rule #4: Don't Be Too Busy to Do the Things You Need to Do to Be Successful.

Hey, we've all blown it like that. I'm just trying to make a point here. Get lucky. Call now. I'm probably the all-time chump in the blowing-the-lead department.

One day, I was doing one of my favorite things, seeing an FSBO, and I had worked up a good rapport. The guy actually gave me the names of five transferred buyers who had been by his property but weren't interested in it for one reason or another. I was a very busy guy. I got around to calling those buyers about a week later. I can report that all five had purchased a property in the last couple of days. None of them bought from me, of course. I was too busy. To cap it off, I didn't even ask the addresses of their new purchases so that I could send a bottle of wine to congratulate them and welcome them to the area. I didn't even put them on my mailing list.

Rule #5: Get Lucky

When you're a superstar in real estate, everybody will think you're lucky. Lots of people will tell you so.

Guess what? You are. Isn't it lucky to be successful and make a lot of money?

However, you make your own luck. You do the things successful people do. You don't wait around to get lucky. There is no Real Estate Fairy.

You Can't Sell Them All. Just Act Like It.

Crime number one, on my part, was not following up immediately. Crime number two, and maybe the greater of the two, was not following up after they bought from someone else.

Think about it. If my theory is true that this is a long-term referral business and other agents don't follow up, then who is going to get that buyer's referrals? Why not you?

Remember, I told you the National Association of Realtors says 65 percent of buyers wouldn't deal with their agents again. Listen. That's just the tip of the iceberg. Another 25 percent could care less.

I'm serious. Most buyers can't even remember their agent's name.

Only about 10 percent of homebuyers are happy enough with their transaction and their agent to actively recommend him or her.

Here's the thing. Let's say I did get the addresses of all five buyers. Let's say I did take them a bottle of wine and a big welcome. What are they going to think? They're going to think that I'm some special kind of real estate agent, aren't they?

What about their own agents, the ones who got those big commissions? They haven't even heard from them. Meanwhile, here I am with a bottle of wine.

Those buyers are going to remember me. And they're going to talk about me to their co-workers and friends.

Maybe that's a record. Five blown leads in one day. You know what else? I didn't get the FSBO listing either. Some other broker got it that same day. An agent from my office sold it, that same day. All and all, you might think I had a bad day. I guess I did. However, I learned some very important lessons that I'll pass along to you so you don't have to learn from trial and error, which is the most expensive education of all.

CHAPTER FIVE

How to List FSBOs

I love FSBOs: For Sale By Owner's. FSBOs have been mighty good to me. These people are actually spending their own money advertising and have their own hand-painted signs. Marvelous. They're advertising that they need help. Why don't you be just the one to give it to them?

Major Concept #6: FSBOs Are Advertising for Your Help, Sometimes on Purpose

Sometimes FSBOs are advertising they need help. I rented a house to a little old lady who had just sold her house. I asked her, out of professional curiosity, how she happened to pick the listing agent who had just sold her house.

She said that her husband called her from overseas and told her to sell the house. She agreed but didn't know any agents. She noticed the house across the street was for sale. She walked over and asked her neighbor how they had selected their agent. The neighbor told her about a wonderful way to find an agent. "What you do," the neighbor told her, "is run an ad in the paper that says 'For Sale by Owner.' Then, all these agents come by. You just pick the one you like best."

She ran her ad in the paper. What happened? Nothing. Really. Finally, she looked out her front window and called the fellow whose name was on the sign across the street. Isn't that incredible? This is a true story. She advertised for help and nobody came. Not even me. I was too busy. Are you?

When I was new in the business, driving around with signs on my car, I saw a hand-painted FSBO sign in a yard. Stopped my car. Got out. Walked up to the front door. Knocked. Lady answered, "Yes?"

Talk about quick on my feet. I said, "Uh. Hi. I'm Tom Mourning with Valley Realty. And, uh, I understand you are thinking about selling your house, and I was wondering if I could be of some help to you?"

(Of course you understand she's thinking of selling her house, dummy. You just walked past her sign.)

She said, "You sure can, young man!"

I went in, and she listed the house with me on the spot. What an easy business. Am I lucky!

FSBOs get the greatest agents that way. Maybe that's where my tenant got that great idea. Maybe it had been passed down for years through the neighborhood how this lady got this great agent as an FSBO. Of course, a few years later when my tenant-to-be went FSBO, I was too busy to help her by calling on her ad or stopping at her sign. You shouldn't be.

... And Sometimes Not on Purpose. They Still Need Your Help.

I point out the above so you can believe me when I say that fully 10 percent of all FSBOs are listings just waiting for you to take. How'd you like to get another 20 percent or 30 percent of those you see?

Interested?

The FSBO is the finest, purest sales situation I have ever encountered. Here is a person who has absolutely no intention (except for the 10 percent mentioned above) of listing his house. He thinks it's easy. He thinks real estate agents are idiots and don't do anything to earn those huge commissions. He thinks he can save 6 percent of the price of his house, which may be something like $12,000, a lot of money, thank you very much!

How can you argue with this guy? You can't. Remember Al Tomsic? "Smile and agree, call them by name, and ask questions!"

This is a pure sales situation. You can't tell. You can't debate. You can't argue.

The person trying to sell his own home is misguided to his possible financial peril. And you can't tell him.

However, I do have a script for you.

FSBO Script

When I say script, I mean script. Again, it's like a play. The seller has his lines. You have yours. You will be totally amazed at how good he is at his.

It is important to understand the advantage you have just knowing this.

In order for this little play to take place, you must go to the property. Rule #1: The telephone is only for making appointments. Never try to sell on the phone. Always sell in person, face to face.

You will have no problem getting into the property. Hey, the house is on the market. It's for sale.

You always let them know you are an agent. However, you just might be a buyer. If the price is right, you might be. Besides, it's your job to know the inventory of all the homes for sale.

Even though the seller may think real estate agents are idiots, he is always interested in free marketing information. Often he will try to show off how smart he is. FSBOs usually love to talk about real estate. If the address is in the paper, just go. Don't call. Just go.

If there's no address in the paper, call. Say, "I'm Tom with Valley. Wanted to look at your house. Would fifteen minutes be okay?"

"We're not going to list it!"

"Of course not. No problem. Fifteen minutes okay?"

You see the address in the paper, and you go by. Nobody home. Leave a note on the back of your card. "I just wanted to take a look. Thought it was for sale. Nobody here. Good thing I'm not a buyer. Call me."

Go by every day until you get in. Leave lots of cards with cute little messages. Maybe they'll get the message.

Probably not, as you have to *sell* the FSBO.

Here's how. You go to the door. The homeowners are home. They answer.

You say, "Hi. My name is ____, with _____, and I understand you're thinking about selling your house. I was wondering if I could be of help to you."

They'll probably say something like, "Yes, but we just want to try it for a couple of weeks on our own and see what happens."

You smile and say, "I can certainly understand that. In fact, if I were you, I'd probably be doing exactly the same thing if I hadn't learned what I know now. After all, 6 percent of the sales price of this property is a lot of money, isn't it?"

(Yes, it is!)

"And the general public's idea of what we real estate agents do to earn all that money isn't much, is it?"

(No, it's not.)

(You smile and nod your head yes, look down, and start wiping your feet while going on.) "Would it be possible for me to look at the property? Perhaps I can give you some valuable marketing ideas. No obligation on your part, of course."

What's the homeowner to say but, "Sure, as long as you understand we aren't going to list it."

You reply, "Great. Why don't we look? And, while we're at it, why don't you show me the property exactly how you would like for me to show the property when I bring my buyers through."

(No, you don't have a buyer for this particular property now. Even if you think you might, you don't tell the seller you do. It's a guaranteed short commission. Average agents will sometimes bring their mothers through with the idea that the FSBO will be impressed. Don't. Don't even think of showing the property without first getting a full commission listing, even if the listing is for one party, for one day.)

As you tour the property, take out your legal pad, take notes, react to the property with enthusiasm, and ask questions. If the sellers haven't provided a brochure, ask how much they are asking.

They might respond with, "What do you think it's worth?"

You say, "I really don't know yet. I haven't seen it yet. How much are you asking?"

Remember, this house is supposed to be on the market. Also ask things like how old the property is, how long they've owned it, square footage, bedrooms, baths, age of roof, age of water heater, furnace, and appliances.

Ask, "Where are you headed from here?"

Ask about their current financing and if they'd be interested in carrying a loan on the property.

After your tour of the property, you will return to wherever you began, probably the entryway. The seller will ask what you think. Of course, he wants to know your opinion of the price. This is an FSBO looking for some free marketing help. You are there to help, but not just yet. Besides, it doesn't matter what you think at this point. What matters is that you stick to the script.

You may think the house is $100,000 overpriced. You may think it's the greatest house you've ever seen, that you could sell it in a minute, or would even consider buying it yourself at the price they're asking.

It doesn't matter. You are on stage. You have a role to play. To paraphrase an old joke, a real estate manager says to an agent, "I'm sorry to tell you this, but you need to think about finding another line of work."

The agent, shocked, says, "What, and leave show business?"

Your scripted response to his question, "What do you think?" is, "I think it's great!" How can they argue with that?

All houses are great if they're priced right. Price is the number one factor in selling property. Major Real Estate Myth #2: Location, location, location. Wrong. It's Price, price, price.

One time I took a listing at more than the market value. Put it on broker tour. The agents sniffed and called it a "dog." It was "dirty." It was "poorly decorated." It was on "too busy a street," and on and on. When it didn't sell after being on the market a couple of weeks, I got a $25,000 price reduction, put it back on tour, and the agents thought it was "beautiful!" It sold instantly.

That experience hit me like a lightning bolt. Even sophisticated agents don't always think about a property in terms of price. They think about the size, condition, or location. Those things are important, true, but those things can be adjusted for in price.

If agents don't get it, believe me, average sellers won't, either. It's up to you to educate them. To do that, sometimes I'll even relate the above little story to make the point.

You go on to ask, "Could we go to the kitchen table? I have just a few more questions I need to ask before we can go over the marketing. Okay?"

You go to the kitchen table. (Always use the kitchen table. Not the living room. Not the family room. This is not a social occasion. They might offer you a drink. You may have only water.)

At the kitchen table, you continue, "Mr. and Mrs. ____, I understand you when you say that you want to sell the property on your own. At this point, I am just trying to get some information so I can be of help to you in marketing your property, with the idea that, if your property hasn't sold in two weeks, you'll think of me when it comes time to turn it over to a professional. I have just a couple more questions I need to ask. However, before I do that, let me tell you a little about me, and my company, so you'll know who you're dealing with. Okay?"

You tell them about yourself and your company. Then proceed to the questions. Ask about their timing, their motivation, if a referral is in order out of town, about special features of the property, about improvements they've made since they've owned the property, and the cost of those improvements, and about what they've most appreciated about the home. Take copious notes.

So far, is there anything here that is difficult for you to live with? How do you think the sellers feel so far? Is it possible that they will appreciate your concern and professional attention? Is it possible that you will actually be building rapport here?

Major Real Estate Myth #3: Sellers give agents listings. Wrong. Except for maybe friends and relatives, nobody is ever going to give you a listing. You must earn it.

In the example we're using, the FSBO is neither friend nor relative. The people are not going to give you their listing. As I recall, they just told you that they are not giving their listing to anybody for a couple of weeks until after they've tried it on their own.

You are going to have to earn this listing. In fact, I want you to earn every listing you ever get. I don't ever want you to feel out of control with a listing because you and the sellers feel like you owe them.

This is a sales situation. You can never sell anybody anything unless you first build trust and confidence. Asking questions about a seller's property, taking notes, and taking the time to help them build rapport, trust, and confidence.

The Moment of Truth: The Seven Fears That List

You've met the sellers. You've toured the property. You've asked questions and taken notes. You have told them about your company and yourself. You have built rapport, trust, and confidence. They still, of course, won't list.

However, we're just getting to Act II of what is usually a two-act play.

Act II is The Seven Fears. These are seven questions designed to change the FSBO's way of thinking by eroding the strength of his position.

Actors ask, "What's my motivation?"

Your acting motivation here is not the commission. It is not even the listing. Your motivation here is evangelical fervor, convincing these people that they may be making a very serious mistake in handling what is probably their most important financial asset. They may be in potential financial peril. You must handle this without telling or judging, however. Use your motivation by using the script, which requires, of course, asking questions.

Closing on the Seven Fears

"Closing" is a term used in sales to mean the actions of the salesperson leading the client to sign an agreement. Here is a scenario designed to lead to that action, which throughout this book always means one thing: a question. Obviously, the questions are different in different situations, but they are always exactly the same questions in the same situations.

Here, motivated by evangelical fervor, we are asking questions to erode the FSBOs logical, but fatally flawed, position. We listen after every question carefully to see if concern has yet entered their consciousness. When we think it has, we close.

The FSBO closing question is, "Why don't you turn it over to a professional?"

The unspoken subtext to this question is, "I understand why you thought of attempting this on your own, but it is dangerous for you to attempt it, and there is no upside for you anyway. Any reasonable buyer will want to save the commission. I just want you to turn it over to a professional, any professional, to protect you and net you the highest possible price, in the least amount of time with the least inconvenience to you. By the way, since I'm here (and since your Uncle Charlie who is a part-time agent in the next county forgot to explain all these financial downsides to you), why don't we get started right now?"

Fear #1: Do You Have a Deposit Receipt?

The text to all of the seven fears is a helpful, concerned question. The subtext is, "Do you have a clue about what you are doing here?"

The deeper subtext is, "I am here to help."

If the FSBO says yes, you should say, "Great. Do you know how to fill it out?"

If he says no, say, "Would you like to have one? I have one in the car. Would you like for me to show you how to fill it out?"

You listen to the response. As a practical matter, I've never been able to close on the first fear. I go on, without closing.

Fear #2: Do You Know How to Qualify a Buyer? Do You Know What Lenders Are Currently Requiring in Terms of Earnings Ratios?

Now listen to the response and, when you notice their knees have not exactly buckled under them yet, go on.

Fear #3: Do You Have the Necessary Disclosure Forms that You, As a Seller, Are Required by Law to Provide Your Buyer?

Listen again. At this point, although you are getting their attention, you can see that their determination has not wavered. Yet. I've never closed one here, either, so go on without closing.

Fear #4: A Motivated Buyer Is in the Market Twenty-Four Hours a Day, Seven Days a Week. I'm Sure You Are Aware of the Hours We Work. Are You Able to Show Your Property to a Prospective Buyer at Any Time?

Listen to the response. Is a little sweat forming on the FSBOs brow? Not yet? Well, it will in a minute. I have closed more FSBOs on the fifth fear than you would believe. The script goes just like this:

Fear #5: I'm Sure You Haven't Thought About This, Mr. and Mrs. Jones, But ...

The very first time this happened to me was on a Sunday. I had just finished my open house, and I had been thinking through a particular FSBO presentation. I couldn't wait to give it a try.

I was driving down the street, and I happened to see a man and his wife standing in their front yard. She was holding a hand-painted FSBO sign in the ground and he, with a hammer in one hand and a martini in the other, was banging the sign into the ground.

I pulled up, got out of the car, walked over, and introduced myself. They were a nice, suburban couple. They were a typical FSBO couple, as well. He wanted to sell the house themselves and save all that money. She had mixed emotions about it, but was willing to give it a try since he felt so strongly about it. Of course, the fact that he was going to be at work all day, leaving her in charge, concerned her.

We went through the scenario as described above, exactly. Act I, Scene I, we toured the property. Scene II, they invited me into the living room and offered me a martini. I suggested the kitchen and a few questions. In the kitchen, with a glass of water, I told them about my company and me and asked questions. Act II, Scene I, I went through the first four fears as described above. Then came Act II, Scene II, and "The Close." It happened to come at Fear #5.

I said, "Mr. and Mrs. Jones, I know you hadn't thought about this, but ..."

"Mr. Jones, you just hammered that sign in the front yard. Tomorrow, you are going to get into your car and go to work. Mrs. Jones will be here, alone. A car drives down the street. It stops. A man gets out. He walks to the door. He says he is a buyer and asks if he could look at the house. Now, Mr. Jones, what is your wife going to do?"

I paused for a second to let the implication sink in. Then I said, "She's going to let that stranger in."

"I'm sure you hadn't thought about this," I said. "Why don't you turn it over to a professional?"

I looked at them and didn't say one more word. You could have cut the tension in the room with a knife. I waited. It seemed like someone had turned the thermostat to one hundred degrees. I kept waiting. It was probably less than a minute, but it seemed like forever.

Rule #2: After Asking a Closing Question, the First One to Talk Loses.

Finally, Mrs. Jones broke the silence. "You know, George, he's right. We *didn't* think about that. Let's get this property listed with this nice young man right now!"

They listed it with me. Not the agent who lived next door. Not their Uncle Charlie, a part-time agent who would have shaved the commission for them. No, they listed it with me. They listed it with me because I was the one who cared enough to educate them as to the possible consequences of their actions. They listed it with me because I asked them to turn it over to a professional, and they did.

They weren't the only ones. Time after time, after the fifth fear, the wife would utter those lines, just like she had been practicing her script all night. No matter how many times it happens, pull out that listing agreement, fill it out, get it signed, and get this overwhelming feeling of satisfaction of a job well done. A job done like that is a job well done.

Sometimes, it doesn't get done. Sometimes the FSBOs are tough, and even after the fifth fear, they'll still look at you and say, "Yes, but we still want to try it for a couple of weeks on our own and see what happens." Incredible.

Don't get mad. Don't lose it. Simply go on to the sixth fears, which are really a series of questions to which the FSBOs won't have answers.

Fear #6: "Are You an Attorney or a Real Estate Broker? Do You Believe That You Are in the Strongest Possible Position by Negotiating Directly with a Buyer? Do You Think Buyers Will Be Willing to Tell You What They See as Wrong with the Property So You Can Take Their Objection, Handle It, and Close on It? Do You Know How to Open an Escrow? Do You Know What to Do When You Get a Low Appraisal from the Buyer's Lender? Do You Know What to Do When You Get a Questionable or a Conflicting Inspection Report from the Buyer?"

As you can see, with the sixth fear, you can go on and on. Maybe you can just wear them down. Nevertheless, if the seller holds firm after each time you ask him to turn it over to a professional, go on.

Fear #7: Shoes from Cincinnati

"Mr. and Mrs. Jones, I would like you, for just a minute, to reverse your role. Pretend you are a buyer," you say.

"Let's say your company has just transferred you here from Cincinnati, and you're on your house-hunting trip. This is the third home you've had to purchase in your moves. You know the ropes."

"You know, for instance, that you could call me, and I'd pick you up at the airport, buy you lunch, and show you the absolute best properties on the market in your price range. You know that I would make sure you got a fair deal and take care of all of the details like inspections, financing, and escrow."

"No. You don't choose to take advantage of my services. You fly into town. At the airport, you purchase all the local papers, rent a car, get a map, and go to your hotel. There you look through all the papers' classified ads, circling the FSBOs of interest, call them, make appointments, route out your travels on the map, look at homes, and make an offer on the one you like best, not really knowing if the price is actually fair or not."

"Have you got the picture, Mr. Jones? Do you see yourself out there wheeling and dealing? Okay, now tell me, why are you going to all this trouble and taking all this risk? Why?"

Wait for an answer.

"That's right, Mr. Jones. You are going to all that trouble to *save the commission*. Are you aware, Mr. Jones, that over 90 percent of all home sales are completed through real estate brokers? Do you know why? It's because the average FSBO sells his house at 10 percent below market value."

"Do you know what the FSBO says to himself when he finally accepts the low offer? He says, 'Oh well, I would have had to pay a real estate broker anyway.'"

"So, Mr. Jones, the FSBO has risked his most important financial asset and risked running into some real bad folks out there. All for what? To save the buyer the commission. Why? Why don't you turn it over to a professional?"

Do you see the logic? Is it irrefutable? Of course it is. There is no way a reasonable person would not have his confidence absolutely shattered and list with you on the spot.

Yet, sometimes, on very rare occasions, you can actually find someone who defies all logic and doesn't list with you. They blow their lines right at the climactic ending. Guess what happened?

Epilogue: You Can't Get Them All, but It's Worth Trying.

Remember I told you about the FSBO who gave me five leads, and I blew them all? I didn't even get the listing. Another broker got the listing, somebody in my office sold it the same day, and the other broker got a full-listing commission for ten minutes of work. Remember I said I learned a lesson? Here's what happened.

This FSBO and I had great rapport. I toured the property, went to the kitchen table, told about my company, asked the questions, and went through the fears. All seven of them. When he said, "Yes, but I just want to try it for a couple weeks on my own and see what happens," I was shattered. I could not believe it. I left with my tail between my legs.

Now, I'll never say you will get them all. However, when you have the rapport, when you have the chance to put on a full presentation with a reasonable person, and still you don't get the listing, it is surprising.

The follow-up script with a stubborn FSBO who refuses to list with you is to return to the house every day. And every day, you ask, "Did you sell your house yet?"

In the example of my FSBO with five leads, I called on this fellow the very next day. "Did you sell your house yet?"

He said, "Well, as a matter of fact, I did!"

I was standing at his front door when we had this conversation. I think he might have had to throw a bucket of water in my face to revive me. When I recovered, I asked, "Really. What happened?"

He said, "Well, right after you left, this old broker came by. He started going through this same stuff you and I had just gone through. I told him about our discussion and said I still wanted to try it on my own."

"He asked me if I had ever heard of an Exclusive Agency listing. I hadn't. He explained that an Exclusive Agency listing is where, if the seller sells the house on his own, he doesn't have to pay a commission. However, if the broker or any other broker sells the property, the seller does have to pay a commission. He asked me if I'd be interested in listing on that basis. I asked where to sign. Well, it wasn't but a few minutes later that a woman from your office brought a buyer through and wrote a contract. She and the other broker presented it. I took it. And, well, there you are."

Sadder but wiser, indeed. Now you know about Exclusive Agency listings and the FSBO. With just two admonitions, however.

First, never take the agency listing without first going through the whole play, including the seven fears. You will get an amazing number of people agreeing to list after that presentation. Why take an agency listing unnecessarily?

Second, always structure the agency listing so it becomes an Exclusive Right to Sell in two weeks. Remember the FSBO said he just wanted to try it for a couple of weeks.

Here's how to do it. Just use a regular listing agreement. When you come to space with room to write in the agreement, say to the seller as you are writing, "Here's how I write up my Agency listings."

"This is an Exclusive Agency Listing until midnight, (date two weeks later), after which time it will become an Exclusive Right to Sell listing and will go on the multiple listing service (MLS)."

The reason my sellers like this is they can go to their prospective buyers and honestly tell them they have two weeks to get their offer together or they are going to have to pay a commission.

The Care and Treatment of Decision Makers

Rule #3: 90 Percent of the People in This World Can't Make a Decision. Don't Ask Them to Do So.

Only 10 percent of the people you will deal with can make a decision. You know who they are. They are usually quite wealthy. They are the buyers who tell you, "Write it up!"

Naturally, if we had to depend on that, 90 percent of the time we would go broke. Ninety percent of the people you deal with have to think about it. All the presentations in this book are designed with that 90 percent in mind, including the above presentation.

You have to treat the decision maker differently.

The largest single transaction I ever did was with a client I acquired as an FSBO. Decision makers don't usually do FSBO. When they do, you'll notice a difference.

I remember that day. It was a Saturday. I looked up from my busy work, realized that I was falling short of my plan, and I needed a transaction immediately. I told myself to go see some FSBOs.

I picked up the paper. In the classified section was a very professional ad that ended "For Sale by Owner." It gave the address, so I got in my car and drove over. There was a professionally painted sign in the yard. I walked up to the door and knocked. A very sharp, younger guy answered, introduced himself, shook my hand, asked me in, handed me a professionally printed brochure on the property, and asked if I would like to see the house.

He took me through the house, selling his socks off about all the features, the great things he'd done to it, how his family loved it, the great neighbors, how sixty-five agents had already been through and loved it, and on and on.

I said to myself, "Wait a minute. What's going on here?"

I must have looked confused because he stopped and asked, "Anything the matter?"

I said, "Boy, you sure look familiar."

He didn't look familiar in the sense that I knew him personally. I didn't. He looked like somebody I'd met before. A decision maker. Once you've seen one, you'll never forget it.

He responded to me by saying, in essence, that he was a famous guy, owned a big real estate development company, belonged to all the clubs and maybe we'd met.

No, I'd never met him. I knew who he was. I'm not sure what came over me, but I said to him, "What the heck are you doing? Are you doing all this to save a lousy $21,000? I mean, look, you could be out on the golf course with your buddies tomorrow hatching a $100-million-dollar deal and you're sitting here trying to sell a house? What are you, nuts?"

He looked at me. His mouth fell open. His face got red. He started to talk. I interrupted, "Look. I'll tell you what. Why don't you go play golf with your buddies tomorrow? I'll hold the house open. If I sell it, you'd pay me the $21,000, wouldn't you?"

He looked at me, stuck his hand out, and said, "You've got a deal."

Next day, I held the house open. Another agent brought a buyer through and wrote a contract. We presented it to the seller's happy, sunburned face that evening. He signed. He thought I walked on water.

He went on to list eleven houses with me in one of his subdivisions. I sold half of those myself. He thought I was special. He told me he had this piece of land and asked if I'd try to sell it for him. I listed it and sold it myself for full price in a couple of weeks. This all happened in about ninety days.

That was one of my better FSBOs. You can see why I love them.

As a final thought about FSBOs, be sure to ask for referrals. Nobody, absolutely nobody, knows more people thinking about buying or selling than our friend, the FSBO.

CHAPTER SIX

Working with Builders, the Ultimate FSBOs

When I was new to the business, I didn't have a client base and didn't know about WDYK. I didn't want to knock on doors, I couldn't afford to send out newsletters and wait two years for a response, I didn't know about cold calling, and I couldn't be on floor time all the time.

After some thought, I decided to put Valley Realty signs on my car doors, drive around, and become an expert in the inventory of potential houses on the market. I also decided to see FSBOs. I reasoned they must be motivated sellers if they spent money advertising and went to the trouble to paint a sign for the front yard.

It turned out that the ultimate FSBO was the builder.

I've mentioned the first time I worked with a builder. I was driving around one day, when a spec home builder noticed my signs and waved me down. A spec home is a house built on speculation and usually not sold until it is completed, as opposed to a custom home, which is built to the customized plans of a buyer.

The builder finances the spec home construction. The buyer usually finances a custom home's construction. Many small homebuilders prefer to build on speculation as they don't have to deal with a buyer during the building process.

This spec homebuilder waved me down and asked if we were the agents who had the lots on the golf course listed. I replied that indeed, we were, and in fact, I even had the maps right here on my car seat. I asked what he'd like to know.

He wanted to look at the maps and the lots. He wanted to buy one.

Talk to Your Local Banker

The only problem was he had all of his capital tied up in the spec home he was currently building. I asked him if he owned his own home. I made an appointment to see his home to see what kind of equity we had to work with in the future.

I took the listing, and the next day, took him down to a local banker to explain the situation.

You need to meet your local bankers. Not the big banks. The big banks finance the big builders. The little local banks have construction loan programs for the small builders. Have the local banker explain to you how the construction loan process works. Typically, the bank will require plans and cost estimates and will loan on the entire construction cost, requiring the builder to come up with the cost of the lot. Sometimes they will even finance all, or part, of the lot cost, depending on the strength of the builder's credit and his track record.

On the other hand, like this particular banker, they might loan the entire amount, cross-collateralized against equity in other property. When I took my builder to the bank, I came armed with comparable sales figures I had used to take the listing. The banker was happy to loan this builder 100 percent of the lot and construction cost of the golf course house by using the equity in his residence as additional collateral.

I sold him the lot, listed his home, and listed the spec home on the golf course. It was the most expensive listing in our office at the time. One day, a stockbroker called me. He'd done a WDYK and gotten my name from a mutual acquaintance. I bought some stock from him, WDYK'd him, and found out he wanted to sell his house. I listed his house and started looking for his next home. He wanted something new, something big, and, hopefully, something on a golf course. Eureka!

The commission on that home was huge. And it was fun. That sale began a long and mutually profitable relationship with that builder as well as other builders in the area.

Just like FSBOs, I found them by driving around and reading their ads in the papers. Just like FSBOs, they found that, without good agent representation, they alone carried all the risk and liability, and they wound up giving the commission to the buyer anyway.

Agents and builders have kind of a love–hate relationship. They love you when you sell their house. They hate you when they figure out that you made more money on the transaction than they did. They spend three to six months of their lives on the building project. They take the risk. They invest the money. After they figure out their wages, they look at their profit, and then they look at the commission they're paying you.

It's natural they should feel this way. You can't argue with their logic. Suggest to them that maybe they should get a real estate license.

Maybe they'll find out it isn't quite as easy as it looks. Alternatively, maybe you should go out, get a contractor's license, and build your own spec houses. Maybe that's not as easy as it looks, either!

Work With On-Site Builder Agents

On larger projects, builders like to have their own on-site agents. They tell me that if there are twenty or more homes, it is usually worthwhile. Builders usually pay on-site agents one to 1.5 percent commissions against a guaranteed monthly draw. They will often cooperate with resale agents, paying them 3 to 4 percent or a flat fee for bringing their agent a buyer. The builder, of course, pays for all the marketing, brochures, flyers, price sheets, plans and elevations, advertising, and model homes.

One day, I was touring some model homes, picking up brochures and price sheets for my files, when I stopped to chat with the on-site agent. I had sold some of her homes before.

She told me the subdivision was nearly sold out, and she would be moving on to a new one. I asked her how the builder planned on marketing the remaining homes and models. She said he would list them with a good resale agent. She introduced me to the builder, and I got the listings. I got a full commission. Only this time, instead of listing just one house, I listed six at one time.

I agreed to hold them open every weekend. Knowing what I know today, I would have moved my office into the model and held them open every day.

Pre-Sell Model Homes to Investors

After having a taste of six listings at once, I began to work more and more with builders. One day, while touring a model complex, the on-site agent told me that the builder was planning to sell the models to investors. He explained to me the builder usually did that to free up his credit line. He was going to sell them at the same price as the rest of the homes, throwing in the cost of the furniture, decorating, and landscaping.

The builder would lease them back from the investor at the investor's cost of principle, interest, taxes, and insurance (PITI) and would pay for all maintenance for two years. The upside for the investor was potential appreciation (a likely scenario) and the tax write-off available for depreciation. At the end of two years, the builder would have no further obligation and the investor could rent them to someone else, sell them, or move into one of them.

This was a very good deal. I called all my investors and found one who was interested. I wrote the offer. The investor was going to buy all four and planned to move into one, or more, in two years. He thought his kids might want to live next door. I took the offer to the builder. He loved me.

I asked if he had any more subdivisions that he might need help with. In fact, one of his on-site agents had just left him. He wondered if I wanted to work on-site. I explained that I had worked with a number of builders and how I worked with them. On a large subdivision like the one we were talking about, I would staff the project myself. Either I would be there every day, or I would hire someone to staff it. I would work the resale agents, selling them on showing his fine product. I would take a 6 percent commission, paying 3 percent to other agents if they sold the property and only 5 percent if I sold it myself. He would continue to pay for flyers, price sheets, model maintenance, and advertising.

Can you imagine? I walked into my office. My colleagues were having a meeting. I apologized for being late. I explained that I had been out taking a listing. Well, actually, I had been out taking thirty-one listings. Incredible!

Work with Big Builders in Buyer's Markets

The real estate market runs in cycles. Sometimes homes sell like hotcakes. This is called a seller's market.

In a seller's market, builders sometimes have people camping out the night before the opening to get in line to buy a house. In a market this hot, builders often reason they don't need me. In fact, they often won't even cooperate with resale agents in hot markets. You know what? They're probably right. Why pay me a full commission, when they can sell their houses all day long. All they need is an order taker working on a 1 percent commission.

However, sometimes, homes don't sell like hotcakes. Sometimes the houses just sit. This is called a Buyer's Market. No lines. No waiting. The builder now has a problem. He is paying some order taker a draw for sitting on his models. The houses aren't selling. His overhead keeps running, nevertheless. Builders call it, "Eating your arm to survive."

Now he needs you. First, you'll see them start to offer resale agents a cooperating commission. Then, you'll see them start to list with the resale agents to cut the monthly overhead.

Do Your Own Price Analysis

Builders are just like any other sellers. They have preconceived notions about how selling houses works. They think, "Location, location, location."

You know better. You know to think, "Price, price, price."

They think selling is telling. They think advertising sells houses. They think that if they run a half-page ad on Sunday in the local paper that people—buyers—will come. They think that if you tell the people all the good features of the house correctly, they will buy. They don't know a "buyer pool" from a swimming pool.

I ran into one builder who wanted me to list his thirty-six-unit subdivision, where he had sold only three in three years. I asked him if he saw a problem. He said he had a rotten on-site sales agent, and the houses hadn't been marketed correctly. He was getting rid of his agent and getting a new ad agency.

I told him I would do a study of the situation and get back to him. He had four floor plans with a couple of elevations each. Each plan had a price. The homes were all completed and sitting there, meter running.

Studying the price sheet and walking the houses, I found that since the houses were all priced the same, some of the lots were far superior. The houses on the best lots were actually a bargain while the houses on the poorest lots were over-priced.

I put my own prices on the individual houses, raising prices on the best lots and lowering them on the worst. This made the houses on the worst lots the lowest priced new homes in the area.

I went to the builder and explained my reasoning. I advised him to re-price the houses and run a half-page ad emphasizing the new pricing. Naturally, we disclosed the number of homes available at those prices and that the prices varied, depending on the lot size and view. I took thirty-three listings.

The ad broke the following Saturday. When I drove up to the model complex, there were people already waiting. I told my on-site agent to hand a flyer, price sheet, and subdivision map to each person or couple and explain that I would be happy to meet with them and answer their questions. First, however, I wanted them to pick out the house they were interested in. I explained that we'd hate for them to lose out on their house just because they were talking to me. I told the agent to suggest that they pick out a second choice, in case their first choice had been already sold by the time they got back. People sometimes looked at her as if she was a little odd, but they also got excited.

Talk about excited. How do you think I felt? That night, I called the builder at his home.

"Well, did you sell one today?" he boomed.

I had to chuckle, "Nope."

I paused.

"I sold NINE!" Wahoo!

Nine sales in one day is my personal record. The thirty-three houses all sold in three weeks, also a personal record.

It all happened because I was unwilling to accept the builder's pricing. I insisted that we price the houses to reflect the difference in lot values. He had paid the same for each lot. He didn't even think of the difference in value because there was no difference to him in his cost.

The lower prices on the poorest lots attracted lots of attention, but they were the last homes to sell. With the builder's old pricing program, these homes were astoundingly overpriced. Their poor pricing affected the whole subdivision's appeal in a very negative way.

Build Them Yourself in a Seller's Market

Builders are fabulous clients. They are motivated. Selling their houses is their business. But they really don't know how. They need your help, especially in a buyer's market.

What do you do in a seller's market? The small builders still need you. The big builders may think they don't need you, but they do. I've seen builders tragically under-price homes in a seller's market. One time, I didn't get the listing, so I bought thirteen homes from a builder. I moved into one and sold the others for a big profit.

As you work with different builders, you'll begin to see that some builders are able to complete their homes at a much lower cost than others. They do this by paying very careful attention to detail.

Some builders recognize the cost of their time investment. They have every detail worked out so the house is built in the minimum possible time. If they price the property correctly, it will sell before completion and close the day it is finished, saving enormous carrying costs and maximizing profits.

In a seller's market, find one of these builders, buy a lot, and pay him a flat fee to build you a spec house. Use one of his standard floor plans. Watch it. Price it right. You will better than offset any lost income from big builder listings.

CHAPTER SEVEN

Open House and the Farm

Farming means specializing in a small segment of a market, generally a subdivision or other geographically contiguous area of one hundred to one thousand homes. What this typically means is the agent will send out a newsletter once a month to home owners in this area advertising his services. Then he waits for people who want to sell to come to him. His usual wait is about two years.

I don't farm.

Not that farming doesn't work, it does. It just normally doesn't work well enough to get that sale this week. My guess is that 80 percent of the people who farm only get three or four listings in their farm a year; 10 percent will get ten or so. However, 10 percent will get 80 percent of the listings in their area and do very well.

What's the difference? The major difference is technique. The secondary, but equally important, difference is turnover.

In some newer areas of the country, one out of five homes can turn over in a year. In older, more established areas, only one in twenty or thirty homes will turn over in a year.

The major difference of technique that successful farmers use is a form of WDYK and cold calling, along with a monthly newsletter and seeing every FSBO and expired listing in their area. Typically, the successful farmer will send out a card to the entire area, in addition to the newsletter, every time he gets a listing or a sale in the area, which is at least once a week.

One of the most successful farmers I ever met worked an area of 485 three-year-old homes reselling in the low $400,000s. When I met him, he told me that he was getting over 80 percent of the listings in his farm. I found that phenomenal.

After some quick calculations, I told him that if one in seven turned over, that was over sixty-nine properties. Eighty percent of that equaled fifty-five sales. Fifty-five sales at $400,000, with a 3 percent commission, equaled more than $660,000 in gross commissions. He said, "That's probably about right, but I sold about seventy last year."

I was stunned. However, I wasn't too dumbfounded to ask how he did it.

He told me, "Well, first of all, that's all I do. Any other business comes my way, I refer it out."

Think about that one. He will not take a listing or work with a buyer outside his farm. Does he focus, or what?

This is an extremely important point. (See Key to Selling Success #1) Let's make it Rule #7: If It's Not in Your Area of Specialization, Refer It Out.

"Second, I hold an open house in my farm *every day*!" he said.

He went on to tell me that every day, he put up open house signs. Every day as residents drove in and out, they would see what a hard worker he was. Every day he was advertising to those residents that he was, in fact, specializing in their neighborhood. On his days off, or when he was on vacation, his full-time assistant would hold the house open for him.

"And, oh yes. Last year, I bought a house in my farm to use as a permanent open house, like a model home. I spot furnished it and put in my whole office with a phone, a fax, and a copy machine. I went to the original builder and got some of his marketing materials, which I put up on easels around the house: pictures of the different elevations of the five different floor plans; an aerial photograph showing the surrounding schools, churches and shopping; a subdivision map showing the layout of the lots and which floor plans were on which lots," he explained.

"On these materials, I put little pins with green showing the homes for sale and red showing the homes I've sold. I can show people how many times I've sold each home. It works pretty well. This way, I'm more organized, I don't have to keep making arrangements with my sellers, and they don't have to be bothered with an open house, just a showing when I find the right buyer."

I was impressed. However, I questioned whether this all really worked. Late one Friday afternoon, he came into my office. Thinking I'd be a wise guy, knowing it was Friday, I asked, "How'd it go in the farm today?"

"Pretty good," he said. "I sold three."

Major Concept #7: Motivated Buyers and Sellers Are in the Market Seven Days a Week—All of Them Are Good Days for an Open House

What this means is that if you are not doing floor time in your office, showing property, or out on a presentation, you should be holding an open house. Drinking coffee and touring property with your fellow agents will not make you a thin dime. If you need to preview property, beyond the four you should schedule to see every day, take one of your unmotivated clients along with you. Who knows, maybe they'll buy one. I can guarantee you that the agent friend you regularly tour with won't buy one from you. After I had a chance to digest what my farmer friend told me, I held an open house every day for two years. I had a full-time assistant to help me on weekends, holding the houses open on my days off and when I was on vacation. What happened? For those two years, I won the "Number One in the Nation Award." Lucky? I got lucky and listened to a guy who told me how he did it, and I tried it myself. Guess what? It worked. It worked so well that, when I went to my company quarterly award breakfasts, I often won every award. The agents would call them the "Tom Mourning Breakfasts!"

The average agent holds an open house once or twice a month on a Sunday afternoon. My best day ever was a Saturday. I sold nine houses. I'm sure glad I didn't wait until Sunday afternoon. I believe I sold as many houses during the week as on weekends. Sure, most of the traffic is on weekends. However, because I was there every day, they often bought it from me the middle of the next week.

Working Open Houses

Let me repeat. When you are not taking floor time, showing property, presenting offers, or putting on a listing presentation, you should be holding an open house.
The house should be

1. In your specialized marketing area;

2. Well priced;

3. Decent in "curb appeal" (a nice enough appearance from the street to prevent "turnarounds," people who don't like the way it looks from the street and turn around and go elsewhere);

4. Where you have at least a phone and a table from which you can work, making your follow-up and WDYK calls and writing contracts. Buy a cellular phone and carry a table and chairs in your trunk.

What else is there to do besides hold an open house? You could always go out and knock on doors. On the other hand, maybe you should find an average agent and find out what he does when he is not showing or writing. Then don't do that. Hold an open house instead.

Don't hold houses open outside your marketing area. If you do that, you'll develop clients for that area and that will keep you from being in the area where you've chosen to be.

Don't hold a house open if it's overpriced. Clients will perceive you as an overpriced agent. How can you list their house at market price if you are representing something else, which is over market? They want a good deal when they buy. How can they believe they will get a good deal from you if overpriced property is where you want to spend your time?

What if you don't have a listing of your own that qualifies? Sit on some other agent's listing. Believe me, he won't be holding it open every day. You can be sure that, if you get his permission to talk to his sellers and you approach them correctly, they will be thrilled. In the meantime, do everything you can do, to the exclusion of everything else, to get a listing like that of your own.

You'll have neighbors come by the open house. Tell them about your plan. Ask them who they know that might be interested in a unique marketing service like an open house every day. Call everybody you know and WDYK them. If those things don't do it, see every FSBO. See every expired. If that doesn't do it, call all the neighbors and explain your problem.

Pick out houses that qualify from the street, knock on the door, and explain your problem. If the homeowners are not in, leave a note explaining it.

I once read an article in the newspaper. A lady wrote a real estate columnist wondering if she had done the right thing. One day, she came home to a note on the door from a real estate agent, saying she was looking for a property just like this one for a client. The note asked if the homeowner was interested in selling. She was. She sold the house, and then she bought a retirement home from the agent. The columnist said he thought the homeowner and the agent who creatively put together two commissions were both lucky. Get lucky—create your luck.

How do you set up an open house? You must make sure the sellers are prepared. They should be absent. You must put up signs. You can do other things to set the stage and make the home more appealing. Turn on all the lights and put some soft background music on the radio. You can even bake bread in the oven and cook apple cider on the range top. Or put a fire in the fireplace and turn up the air conditioning in the summer. You can hand out and/or send out invitations or place an ad. Blow up balloons. Hire a sky writer, a clown for the kids, and a caterer for the parents.

Make a list of the things you want to do for your open house. Make an opening and closing checklist. Give a copy of it to the seller. Then do it.

Then pick up the phone and start making your follow up, WDYK, FSBO ("How's your open house going today?"), expired ("House open today?"), neighbor ("Come on over!"), and other calls to get that next listing.

Okay. You've planned your open house, put up your signs, and prepared the house. Clients come in. You are on the phone (not watching TV, doing crosswords, reading a novel or the newspaper). You are busy.

With a big smile, wave them in, point to the phone, hold up a finger, then excuse yourself from your telephone call, telling the caller you just had some clients come in.

What happens next depends on how many people are coming through at one time. If there are many, just smile, wave them through, and point to your brochure table where you have your property information, personal, and company promotional materials. Just stand back, observing. The good clients will usually come to you when there's a crowd.

If you think you spot a particularly good prospect or if there is no crowd, walk right over. Say, "Welcome!"

Introduce yourself and your company, and ask their names. I like to pull out a business card, write their names on the back of the card, and stick the card in my pocket. I have this theory that when people ask you for your card, they are dismissing you. Therefore, I never give a prospect my card until I wish to dismiss them.

Ask if the prospect would like you to tell him or her a little about the neighborhood and this property, or if they'd prefer to see the house on their own first. They'll say one of a few things: "Oh, we're just neighbors ..." or "We were just driving down the street and ..." or something similar.

Think about what's happening here. We have (1) a looker, (2) a prospective seller, or (3) a real buyer. How can you tell which it is? Ask questions.

Start with, "Where are you folks from?"

Find out if their home is on the market. Is it listed with a broker? As you listen to them, size them up. Do you like these people? Do they seem to relate at all to you? Most of the time, top open house agents tell me, they either get, or don't get, a connection right away. If they don't get a positive connection, they politely back off, but don't put too much energy into the conversation.

Look for a Positive Connection

If you think you have a looker, find out if they've ever thought of moving. Have they made any offers? If they are sincerely lookers, find out if they have any friends or relatives who might be interested in this house. Tell them about your open house program, and find out if they know of anybody interested in selling who might be interested in a service like this. Tell them about your newsletter, and ask if they'd like to be put on your mailing list.

If you have a prospective seller, make a listing appointment. You've talked, and you feel you have a connection. You know they haven't sold their house and need to sell it before they purchase the next one. Say, "Why don't I come by your house and take a look at it so we can determine about how much equity we have to work with in the future? No obligation on your part, of course. Let's see, I could come by this evening at 7:30 or I'm available next Tuesday. Which would be better for you?"

The subtext here is that you understand they may wish to find their perfect property before they sell, and this is just a service for that future time. What will happen, of course, is they will come to appreciate—from your comments—how much better it is for them to have a sold property when they are negotiating for a new one.

If you have a buyer, sell them the property. A friend of mine has had the most incredible success at open houses. After clients have been through the property, this agent asks with a big grin and lots of enthusiasm, "You folks want to buy a house today? How about this one?"

Sometimes the buyer doesn't want this one. Then what? Once, some prospects walked into my open house so tired, they were sagging. After the welcome and introductions, they said they were from out of town, had been transferred here, and had been looking with an agent for two weeks. They had made two offers and lost both. They had to go home the next day. They were tired, unhappy, and discouraged. I connected.

I asked if they would tell me which two properties they had made offers on. They told me. I knew them both. I didn't even know they had sold.

A Motivated Client Often Knows More about the Current Real Estate Market than You Do!

Based on the two properties they had made offers on, however, I knew exactly what they were looking for without showing them one house. I asked them to sit down and relax for just a minute. I had some very good news for them: I had just last night listed exactly the house they were looking for. It was just down the street. I would just be a minute while I went to the phone to make an appointment for them to see their next home. They connected. It was the start of a great "fanship."

Rule #8: Build a Fan Club

There is an ascending ladder of people you will deal with in the real estate business. From bottom to top, these people are: suspects, prospects, clients, satisfied clients, and fan clubs. Your job is to take them from the bottom to the top.

Do you remember Key #6: Think Referrals, Not Commissions?

And, do you remember Major Concept #3: The Best Client Is the Motivated Personal Referral?

It is in your best interest to make the client's best interest your *only* concern. That means you will go out of your way. It means you don't care about the commission. It means that you will impress your clients so much that they will rave about you. They will not be just satisfied. They will be thrilled, delighted, elated, and ecstatic. They will become your admirers, your buffs, your disciples, and yes, your *fans*!

CHAPTER EIGHT

Other Prospecting Methods

If you've carefully read the chapters on WDYK and FSBO, I'm sure you can understand when I say that was about all I had time to do. Those two prospecting methods turned out to be more than enough to meet my plan.

I had a lot of success with builders also. It's important to remember that I prospected them just like FSBOs, which, when they have their own sales force, they are!

As a manager, and as a person simply interested in success in the real estate business, I have observed agents enjoying superstar results with other forms of prospecting. It's called finding your niche. Do what works for you. Don't try to reinvent the wheel. As you work, you'll find some things come easily and others don't.

Do what comes easiest for you, and then stick with it. Be the expert in whatever it is. You'll know it when you see it. You will feel a sense of confidence about that particular niche. You will say to yourself that there really is no one better in this than you. There may be one or two as good, but there is no one better.

You will, of course, be correct. But because selling comes easy to you, you may mistakenly believe that it is no big deal. In fact, I'm sure you'll feel that way. After all, it isn't a big deal to you.

I'll tell you, though, it sure is a big deal to the marketplace. Remember, I said that superstars often feel they don't do much to earn all that money. That's *it*. It's something they know, they like, and they are interested in. They think, naturally, that everyone else feels the same way. Well, everyone doesn't. Because you do, people will become your fans and will begin recommending you. Buyers will beat down the door looking for your special expertise.

I've seen agents excel because they loved horses and horse properties, small rental units, or lots. One agent specialized in selling lots to people who wanted to build a custom home or to small builders who wanted to build a spec house. One top agent only sold condominiums in one building. He sold over three hundred units in one year.

There are lots of other proven successful ways to prospect. Some of these are: expireds, cold calling, farming, open houses, and floor calls.

Working the Expireds

"Expireds" are people who have had their property listed with a broker, but it didn't sell during the listing period. The listing expired.

Expired calls are successful from my experience in about one in ten cases. Most of the properties have already been re-listed or taken off the market. Sellers of those 10 percent that are left are usually very unhappy campers. In particular, they are unhappy with real estate agents. They don't like you by association.

Sometimes when you call on FSBOs, you will find expireds. These people—whose original listing has expired—figure they can't do much worse than their agent did, and they're planning to save all that money. They are almost right.

An average agent took their listing. They never heard from their agent again. I'm serious. They'll tell you, "We thought we'd at least hear from him when the listing was about to expire. And we didn't." That's sad.

Rule #6: Follow Up.

The National Association of Realtors recommends that you follow up at least once a week. That's a minimum. I recommend that you do it every day.

Think about it.

1.   If you were a motivated buyer or seller, would you appreciate hearing from your agent every day?

2.   Who would you give your referral to, the agent who called you every week or two, or the agent who called you every day?

3.   If you call every week or two, what's your seller's script going to be? Right. "Why hasn't my house sold?" He's going to complain that you haven't run a half-page ad in the *Wall Street Journal*, you haven't held it open every day, and he isn't being represented.

Instead of focusing on the real reason, which is price, you have to make excuses and plead for a price reduction. He'll likely scoff and say, "You haven't even brought me an offer. Bring me an offer and I'll think about lowering my price!"

However, if you call every day to report on the market and find out what showings he had yesterday, it's a different story. Then call after a couple weeks, and ask why he doesn't think his house has sold. Believe me, he'll be the one stammering. He'll probably say, "Do you think maybe we should reduce the price?"

With an expired, you can be almost certain that an average agent took the listing, never followed up, didn't price the property correctly, and certainly didn't make the seller a partner in understanding how the whole process works.

You should always ask an expired, "Would you like to know (me or my company's) difference?"

Put on a real listing presentation.

Then follow up.

Cold Calls

Every average agent will tell you that cold calls do not work in his area. Many of the superstars, and nearly all of the mega-superstars (those doing more than two hundred deals a year) will tell you that they got the majority of their clients from cold calls. Cold calls work. Studies have proven it, time and again. It doesn't seem to matter what time of day or which day of the week you make them or whether you do them in person. They work!

Someone told me the other day that cold calls don't work in their area because that area is so sophisticated. Everyone in the area had answering machines to screen calls. I thought that made sense.

However, the very next day, I was talking to an agent who had already, in less than six months, made $250,000. I asked how he got his business. He said that most came from cold calls. Thinking about my earlier conversation, I declared that it couldn't have been in this sophisticated area.

In fact, he told me, it was. He said he found it much easier to call in the so-called sophisticated area, because there was so little competition.

I never did cold calls, except on FSBOs. I never sold more than two hundred houses in a year, either. My goal was to sell fifty or more. I could do that with WDYK, FSBO, and open houses. I also liked to manage offices. If I wasn't managing, I just took more time off.

The commission from fifty houses fit my lifestyle just fine. I knew that if I wasn't getting fifty listings from those three forms of prospecting, I wasn't doing it right. So I just did those things better. However, if I had known that those three forms of prospecting weren't enough to meet my objective, I would have done things differently. First, I would have prospected expireds. Failing that, I would have cold called. If that hadn't worked, I'd have gotten a "real job."

I don't believe I would have ever gotten a "real job." It is my sincere belief that, even though this business isn't for everybody, anybody can make it with the right attitude and the information in this book.

Working Floor Calls

Rule #9: On a Floor Call, Make the Appointment or Hang Up

This is not the Chamber of Commerce. We are not professional guides or taxi drivers. Our job is to sell property. We're good at it. Because we are good at it, we have lots of demand for our services from people who really need it. We simply do not have the time to work with people unless they really need it and are motivated clients.

We have an obligation to our sellers to show their property only to qualified buyers. We do not give out addresses on the phone. In fact, we do not even show a property unless we have first had a chance to sit down with prospective buyers to qualify them.

You should be very enthusiastic and very busy, almost to the point of frustration. You quite simply do not have time to answer a bunch of questions on the phone. You will be happy to do so when you meet.

The caller, however, wants to eliminate the property on the phone. That's right, eliminate. People call on ads with the mind set that real estate ads embellish the truth, but the house they are calling on just might fit their requirements, so they want to make sure it doesn't so they can go on to the next ad.

The stage is set.

Here's the script:

Prospect:	"Hello. I'm calling on your ad."
Agent:	"Yes, that's a fantastic property. The phone has been ringing off the hook. I am now making appointments to show the property. I'm available at 3:15 or 5:45. Which is best for you?"

Prospect:	"Well, actually, we would just like to drive by. May I have the address, please?"
Agent:	"I wish I could. The sellers have asked that we not give out the address unless we are sure the people are actually qualified prospective purchasers. I'm sure you can understand that, particularly on a property as hot as this one. Which is best for you, 3:15 or 5:45?"
Prospect:	"Believe me, I'm qualified. Where is it?"
Agent:	"I believe you. However, we'll need to meet here first. Which is best for you, 3:15 or 5:45?"
Prospect:	"Does it have (whatever)?"
Agent:	"Did you need (whatever)? Which is best for you, 3:15 or 5:45?" (Pause as if you are about to hang up the phone, which you are.)

"I'll be more than happy to answer any and all of your questions at that time, okay?"

That's it. I couldn't be more serious. When I tell agents to use that script, they look at me like I am out of my mind.

I have to remind them, this is a business. That ad call just cost you or your office about $100. You are going to give away the address? Do you have any idea of the probability of that client driving by and calling you back? It's terrible.

I've had irate people call me, and tell me how my agent wouldn't give out an address on the phone. I'm happy to hear it. Sometimes our sellers call us, pretending to be buyers, just to see if we'll give out their address to perfect strangers.

I'll bet if you were a seller, you'd appreciate our professionalism in screening prospects, wouldn't you?

Is your home currently on the market? No? Maybe I could have one of my top agents drop by your property to give you an idea of the equity you have to work with in the future? Would tonight be convenient?

Top floor agents never take more than a minute or two with an up call.

If you were an unmotivated buyer, would you like that floor call response? Probably not. However, if you were a motivated buyer, you probably wouldn't mind. You're in the market seven days a week (per Major Concept #7).

You see an ad for a property that looks like it might be just what you're look-ing for. You call, and the agent is excited because the phone is ringing off the hook on that listing. What do you think you would do? You'd get excited, too. Instantly, fear and greed would set in. Fear at potentially losing a hot property. Greed in finding a good deal. What would you do? You'd make the appointment.

How to Handle the Appointment

Always meet at the office, at a title company office, or at a local restaurant. Never meet at the property.

Why? If you set up the meeting at the property, you obviously must give the address. You never give out the address. It also could be dangerous.

Remember the FSBO fifth fear? There are some dangerous people out there. Don't invite trouble.

You also risk the caller driving by the listing without you. And it's not fair to the sellers. I've seen hot ads draw crowds like Indians circling the covered wagons in the movies.

The main problem with meeting at the property, however, is that it isn't pro-fessional. You are not going to sell anybody anything unless you first build rap-port, trust, and confidence. Then qualify him. We'll go into length about qualifying in the buyer presentation segment of the book. At this point, just know that without qualifying, you are wasting time, energy, tires, and gasoline!

Know that it's just part of the script that the prospect will do anything possi-ble not to get qualified. It's your role to see that he does, or you don't participate.

Make sure your movie has every scene in every act leading to the ending you want. It's not the prospect's movie. He is free to do as he chooses. For you to be involved, he must choose to do it your way. When an average agent doesn't give out the address and makes an appointment to meet at the office, the prospect comes into the office and impatiently tries to get right back out the door. The average agent usually accommodates him by walking out with him, tucking his MLS Book under his arm. Do you see the problem here?

The prospect won. His role is to avoid getting qualified. He didn't get qualified.

Here's a better script:

| Prospect: | "Nice to meet you. Why don't we just follow you to the property in our own car?" |

Agent:	"Fine. (Big Smile) But, before we go, let's just sit down for a couple of minutes so we can get acquainted, okay?" (Extend arm toward conference room).
Prospect:	"Well, we've got the baby in the car with the engine running, and we really are in a big hurry."
Agent:	"Great. I'd be happy to reschedule for another time that's more convenient for you. My time is quite limited as well. As I mentioned when you called, the phone has been ringing off the hook on this property. I have gotten myself really backed up with appointments. The problem is, the sellers insist we qualify our clients before we show them the property. Why don't you bring the baby in? This will only take a couple of minutes."

Again, I must ask you. Do you think a motivated buyer will appreciate this approach? A client called me one time to complain that they went to a new town, checkbook in hand, called offices, and couldn't get anybody to sit down with them. No one would take the time to learn what they were looking for and make some recommendations. Really. Every agent darted out the door, MLS book in hand, to show these people the one house they'd called about. Imagine.

Major Concept #8: 90 Percent of Closing Buyers Is in Your Qualification of Them.

You must make an appointment and sit down with your prospective buyers before you show the property. If you don't, you stand less than a 10 percent shot at selling them a house. You're far too busy for that. There are people who need your help out there, right now. Find them. Qualify them. Then sell them.

Prospecting: A Summary

Major Concept #5 says that if you are not reaching your targeted level of success, your problem has to be either prospecting or presentation. This is simple and logical. Knowing this, ask yourself how many listing presentations and/or buyer qualifications you've been on in the last week or the last month.

The answer to that question will immediately clarify the problem. Usually it will be clear that you've made too few appointments. Remember, your number one job in this business, or in any other sales business, is finding motivated clients.

There are lots of potential clients out there. However, I've found that for every three clients who say they are buyers, only one actually is. So if you work with everyone who says he's a buyer, you'll be wasting 67 percent of your time.

Your efforts should be spent in finding that one in three who really is a buyer. Work with that person. Forget the other two.

How do you tell who is the real buyer? You can't just ask. You can ask a motivated buyer, "Are you ready to buy today?" He'll probably say he's not, and then wind up buying. You can ask the unmotivated buyer the same. He may say he's ready, but he won't buy.

You can only tell by their situation and their actions. If they "have to buy," then they probably will. If they buy or list after being properly qualified or presented, they are motivated. If they don't "have to buy," they probably won't buy, but they're worth qualifying and showing once. If, after they've been properly qualified or presented and shown two or three of the most suitable properties and they don't make an offer, it's clear that they are wasting your time.

They're wasting your time because there are people out there who do need your help right now. Your number one job is to find them. You must get rid of the 67 percent of the people who waste your time so you can use that time to find those who can use and appreciate your help.

If you don't currently have a motivated client to work with, you must do whatever you can do to find one, to the exclusion of everything else. As a practical matter, if you want to do fifty deals a year, that's just one deal a week. You only need find two motivated clients a week.

For me, the easiest way to get two new, motivated clients a week was WDYK. This prospecting method also gives you the additional advantage of being referred. Major Concept #3 says that the best client is the personally referred motivated client. Personally referred motivated clients are more loyal and more apt to give you subsequent referrals after you do a good job for them.

If you can do your fifty deals a year from WDYK personal referrals, why do anything else? If fifty deals satisfy you, why do more? Forget floor time. Forget open houses. Forget FSBOs, expireds, farming, and cold calling. If you can do fifty deals, and you can do it working four hours a day, five days a week, what's wrong with that? Go ahead; spend more time with the family, your hobbies, travel, whatever. Have a life.

By the way, I know that it is possible to do that. I did it. The secret is scheduling. I would schedule an hour or two a day, just for making WDYK calls. Done right, it's difficult not to get a lead in an hour or two. That means you're getting five or six leads a week. You may even have to cut back your calling or start passing out referrals to your fellow agents. Or you might just have to raise your earnings expectations.

If, however, you don't get enough referrals from WDYK, then you must use other forms of prospecting. As I've said, my favorite alternative form of prospecting is the FSBO. Its fun and challenging, and I find it a great game. The FSBO is also a terrific source of referrals.

If you are doing WDYK an hour or two a day, as well as every time you come into contact with anyone; you're seeing FSBOs; and you're holding houses open every day when you are not showing or writing, you should be meeting your goals. If you're not, you've got a problem.

You're probably not doing it right, according to the methods and scripts provided here. Refine your technique. Keep on trying. You'll get it right if you really try. In the meantime, you are still falling short of the two motivated clients you needed this week. What do you do?

First, do all the expireds.
Failing that, make cold calls.

Personally, I hate the idea of cold calling. However, it can be fun.

The biggest problem in cold calling isn't rudeness; it's getting all those friendly folks off the phone. You will have no problem getting people to allow you to add their names to your newsletter mailing list. In about one in every hundred calls, you'll actually get a lead. It works, but you can see why I'd rather sharpen my WDYK skills. One in three beats one in a hundred by a country mile.

The biggest problem salespeople run into is prospecting effectively. You can count on it being your biggest problem as well.

Usually the problem is quantity, not quality. Sometimes salespeople just don't do enough prospecting. Doing enough will always overcome doing it right. Every time. You can do WDYK letter perfect, but if you never do it, the guy next to you cold calling three hours a night will be the one taking home all the trophies.

As you work, keep the major concepts we've discussed in mind. Remember the Rules. They work. Remember the Ten Keys. Enthusiasm, burning desire, and persistence comprise a full 67 percent of your keys to success. Specialize. Believe.

Work with those Fo Dogs of Fear and Greed. Think referrals, not commissions. Act like a superstar. Act busy.

In addition, for crying out loud, quit selling. Selling isn't telling. Selling is asking questions. Listen to the answers. Don't be thinking about what you are going to say next. Above all, have fun!

Now we understand that prospecting is usually the problem. We know what to do to prospect. We do it. Now what?

Now comes the presentation.

If you went on twenty listing presentations in the last thirty days and still haven't met your goals, we know that the problem is not prospecting. We know the problem must be your presentation.

We have two kinds of clients: buyers and sellers. We have two different presentations, one for each. I call them games. Like the FSBO Game, the Listing Presentation Game, and the Buyer Presentation Game are challenging and fun.

The average agent goes on two presentations a month. He succeeds in one out of four. He's doing half a deal a month, which is six deals a year.

Because you now know how to prospect, plan on doing two presentations a week. If you do just that much, based on averages, you will quadruple your volume: eight presentations a month will get you two deals a month, or one in four.

Now, what we want to do is improve that one-in-four success rate to two-in-four or more. If you have a two-in-four success rate, you've doubled your presentation effectiveness. Also, with the increased prospecting effectiveness, you will now be getting at least four prospects a month. That's a deal a week; fifty homes a year.

Major Concept #5: If Your Level of Success is Below Your Goal, It has to be Either Your Prospecting or Your Presentation

Simple, logical, bottom-line thinking has to agree. Let's say your goal is to have eight listings in your personal inventory. Let's say you currently have two. What's your problem? It's simple. Your problem is six.

Why are you six listings short of your goal? I don't know enough yet, do I? Let me ask a couple of questions. How many listing presentations have you been on in the last week? How many in the last thirty days?

You say you've been on two listing presentations in the last thirty days. (By the way, the average agent goes on about two listing presentations a month and gets the listing on only one out of four of those. Some fun, huh?) If it's true that the problem has to be either prospecting or the presentation, which is it?

The problem here is prospecting. Now, we don't know enough yet to know whether the problem is lack of, or inefficiency in, but we do know it's prospecting.

Alternatively, when you say you have been on one listing presentation every night for the past thirty days, your problem obviously isn't prospecting.

CHAPTER NINE

The Listing Presentation Game

You now know how to prospect. You have done your WDYK and made referral appointments. You have held open houses every day that you haven't been showing or writing. You've contacted FSBOs and expireds and even made some cold calls. You have a listing appointment every night this week. Congratulations!

Let's say our goal is eight listings in our personal inventory. Let's say you have two. What's the problem? The problem is six. You have seven listing appointments. Can you pull this off?

The Listing Presentation Game has two players: you and the prospective sellers. The object of any game is for one of the players to win. To win, you must obtain a market value listing with at least a 6 percent commission for a term of at least ninety days, with VA & FHA terms, if appropriate. You must do this on the first appointment.

The sellers will win if they keep you from getting that listing. If you don't get the listing on the first appointment, they win. Less than 6 percent for ninety days or without appropriate terms, they win. If priced above market, they win.

"Unfair," you say? "Un-level playing field," you argue?

After all, it is their property, and they can do what they want. True. That is their advantage.

What's yours? Your advantage is that you know what you are doing, and they don't. You know, word for word, what they are likely to say. You know all their concerns, fears, and potential objections. The sellers will see you as a guest in their home, not as a player in a game. Knowing all of these things, you can control the situation.

Like any game, how you play determines your success. The techniques you are about to learn seem easy at first. However, few have really mastered these techniques. They can be learned with practice and constant reminders. As I mentioned before, some agents will actually review this stuff in the car right before they make a presentation.

These techniques are not 100 percent successes all of the time. However, they give you the greatest edge percentage-wise. You can't get them all. After all, what kind of game is it if you are assured of winning every time? That wouldn't be any fun, would it?

Average Agent Presentation

I have made much about the maxim that to be successful, you must do what successful people do. Conversely, I have made much of studying what the average agent does, and cautioning you not do that.

So, before we get into how we play the Listing Presentation Game, let's look at how the average agent plays it.

Let's say the average agent gets a referral from his mom. Luckily, by the time he gets around to it, the property is not already listed. He makes an appointment on the phone. That's good. The problem is, he tries to sell on the phone and doesn't get any information on the property before he goes out. Fortunately for him, the sellers simply tell him to come on over.

Since he doesn't get any information on the property, he doesn't do a CMA (a competitive market analysis showing recent comparable listings, expireds, withdrawn, pending, and closed sales in his area). He prefers the two-step method anyway.

He shows up late for his scheduled appointment. The seller greets him at the door. The average agent shakes hands and introduces himself, but doesn't mention his company name. He feels that's unsophisticated.

The seller, standing in the entry, says, "Would you like to take a look at the house?"

The agent tours the property. They return to the entry, and the seller says, "Well, what do you think?"

He means, of course, "What do you think it's worth?"

Our average agent mumbles that he will work up the information for the seller. The agent and seller are still standing in the entry. At this point, the seller will either dismiss him by asking for his card or invite him into the living room for a drink.

In either case, as you can see, there is absolutely no way the average agent is going to win the game according to the rules.

Let's say that the same evening, the sellers had made an appointment with you. You follow the rules of the Listing Presentation Game. Guess what happens when Mr. Average Agent calls the sellers back the next day to make his second appointment? The seller will say, "Oh, didn't you know, we listed the property last night. The agent said he'd call you, and let you know. I guess he hasn't had time to get around to it yet. He said to tell any agents who called that we listed it at $_____, which is a very good price. He said to tell you that you can still sell it and earn a commission. And, by the way, give our best to your mom."

Can you imagine? Mr. Average Agent can still sell it and earn a commission. Can you just imagine his beet-red face? Can't you just hear him fume, "What a rotten business!"

Of course, he's right. For him, it is a rotten business. With any luck at all, he'll soon be out of the business, pumping gas, where he belongs. He certainly doesn't belong in a business where you handle what is, to most people, the most important financial transaction in their lives.

If you want to put a little evangelistic fervor in your life, just think about the average agent. The chances are good that if you don't do everything you can, if you don't prospect and follow up with a great sense of urgency, Mr. Average Agent is liable to wind up with the client. What a disaster that could be!

You think I'm kidding? The horror stories and wreckage are all around us. Just call a few expireds, and ask them what they think of their agent. Boy, will you get an earful. However, watch out. If you call an expired, patiently listen, sympathize, and make an appointment to explain *your* difference. You might just get a listing, a grateful client, and a whole pack of referrals!

Playing the Game

Now you know how not to do it. We know enough by now to know that whatever Mr. Average Agent does, we want to do the opposite. We can also gain some self-confidence in knowing that this is how our competition is doing it.

Here's how we do it. Remember, to win the game, you must get a market value listing, at no less than 6 percent, for no less than ninety days in one appointment!

There are nine steps to a correct, high-percentage presentation. There is a reason for each step and a reason for the sequence.

Step #1: Make the appointment. Both parties must be there. Don't sell on the phone. Gather enough information on the phone call to do a CMA.

Step #2: Do a CMA.

- Pull the detailed listing sheet on the three or four sold and closed properties that are most similar, closest in proximity, and most recent in time (you may need to use current listings instead, in a declining marketplace). These are called comps (comparable sales).

- Take the comps and extrapolate. Compare the features of one against the other, assign a value to these features, and adjust the comps' values accordingly. (Stay in regular touch with local appraisers to stay up-to-date on the actual numbers they are using. Be particularly concerned about incremental square footage values.)

- If you have time, drive by the property beforehand, and order a property profile from your friendly title company.

- Pull together your materials for presenting yourself and your company.

Step #3: Be on time. Introduce yourself and your company at the door. Do not tour the property now. The seller's script says, "Would you like to look at the house?"

Your script says, "Yes, I would. However, before we do, I need to ask you some questions about the property in order to give you the highest possible market evaluation. Could we sit down at the kitchen table so I can take some notes?"

Don't sit in the living room or in the family room. Sit at the kitchen table. As a second choice, sit at the dining room table. The seller may offer you a drink. You may have water only. Living rooms and soft music are for emotion, for the buyer. Buyers buy on emotion. Kitchens are where family decisions are made. The kitchen table is hard, cold, logical, and businesslike. Sellers list on logic, not emotion.

Step #4: Go to the kitchen. Sit at the head of the table. Get your materials organized, lean back and say, "Mr. & Mrs. Jones, before I start to ask you my questions, let me tell you a little about myself and my company, so you'll know with whom you are dealing."

Do that.

Step #5: Ask a lot of questions. How long have the homeowners owned the property? What did they pay for it when they bought it? What improvements have they made since they purchased it, and what did each item cost? Take notes on a legal pad.

Ask questions about the information you need to fill out the MLS card. Ask the age of the appliances, the hot water heater, the furnace, and the roof.

Take notes as you listen to the answers. When you talk and somebody takes notes, doesn't that make you feel important? Could you begin to warm up to that person? Are we building a little rapport here?

Motivation? "Where are you folks headed from here?" is the correct script. Do not ask, "Why are you selling?" unless you get perverse pleasure in seeing some people cry.

Timing? When do they need to be where they are headed? Is a referral needed? Are there tax issues? Are there financing issues?

Price? What do they think the property is worth?

They'll tell you, "That's why we asked you over."

They'll ask you what you think it's worth. You don't know. You haven't seen it yet. See why we don't tour the property first?

Your script is, "Mr. and Mrs. Jones (MMJ), I know everyone has an idea as to what their property is worth. It won't affect my evaluation, but I was just curious as to what was your idea of your property's value."

Primary Sales Feature? Script: "I would like for you to tell me what it is about the property you have most enjoyed. Some people say they like to sit out in the backyard and watch the sun set in the evening. Some say they love the sun streaming in the kitchen window with their cup of coffee in the morning. I'd like you to tell me what you've most loved about the property, so *when I bring my buyers through*, I can tell them."

Okay to tour now? Your last question is an assumed close and a definite positive response from the prospect.

"Well, MMJ, I think that about takes care of all my questions. Do you think it would be all right if we looked at the property now? And, by the way, I would really appreciate it if you would both take me through it just like you would like me to show the property, *when I bring my buyers through*."

A potential problem may occur if one of the sellers decides to duck out and catch up on the ball game. You want to keep everyone involved, so ask them both to show you through the house.

Step #6: Tour the property. Be enthusiastic. Make a list of things that need to be done to optimally stage the property. After you tour, always return to where you began. You want to return to the kitchen, not the entry. That's another reason you go first to the kitchen table.

Step #7: Get agreement on the price. When you return to the kitchen table, the seller will probably ask what you think. Now that you've had a chance to build a little rapport, you're much better able to deal with the price issue, which is probably the most important aspect of the presentation. Here is the critical script:

"MMJ, how would you like to help me determine the highest possible market value on your property?"

Would they like to influence your judgment, if possible? Of course. An agent came to me and said he tried that script, and it didn't work. Really, how interesting. I asked what he said. He said, "How would you like to help me ...?" They said that they really didn't want to help him. It was his job, and he was making all this money on their sale. That's why they asked him to the house.

The listing presentation is all about price agreement. You must make the sellers feel like insiders. When you ask for their help, it's not because you want their help. It gets them involved. This question has a harmonious, almost conspiratorial tone, to it. It's you and them against the market. Would they like to participate? Would they like to get their two cents worth into the pricing? You bet they would.

Would they like to help you do your job? I don't think so.

However, they would definitely like to help you determine the highest possible market value on their property. You've got their interest.

Pull out your CMA and your full listing sheets with all the extrapolations on them. Review each of them, item by item, adding and subtracting from the prices as you go. Get price agreement, line item by line item.

The seller may say, "You've given us only $15,000 for our pool. It cost us about $30,000."

You say, "Good point. Appraisers in our area give only about 50 percent of cost on pools."

You're educating them.

On the other hand, the seller may say, "Listen, I paid for that pool. That pool cost a solid $85,000."

You say, "That's a good point. Let's change the extrapolation from $15,000 to $42,500."

You want harmony and agreement. You are not stuck. You want to get them the highest possible—and the most realistic—price you can.

Alternatively, the seller may say, "Honey, the Smith house sold for $300,000. They told us it sold for $325,000!"

Frequently, sellers mistakenly value their properties based on misinformation from neighbors. Your statistics in black and white usually make for a quick awakening from these pipe dreams.

Probably the biggest single mistake agents make in pricing property is improper accounting for incremental square footage. Extra square footage simply doesn't cost as much as initial square footage. If you have a good solid comp with 2,500 square feet that sold for $250,000, or $100 per square foot, what's a 3,000-square-foot home with exactly the same amenities worth? $300,000? Wrong. The incremental square footage is only worth about $30 per foot. For 500 square feet, that's $15,000. Not $50,000.

A contractor and I built a spec house. We took plans for a 3,200-square-foot house and expanded it into 4,200 square feet. Our final cost for that extra square footage was only $2,000. There were no extra kitchens and baths, just a little lumber and sheetrock. Find out from a local appraiser what he uses for incremental square footage in your area for various ages of properties.

Always remember to think, "Price, price, price."

Relocation firms that typically obtain two appraisals for each transferred employee consider 5 percent the maximum allowable difference in appraisals. If two appraisals are more than 5 percent apart, a third appraisal is required.

You've now gone over three or four recent comps and extrapolated them, item by item. You've done it together. You have agreement, item by item. These items add and subtract from the comp sales price, leaving you with a bottom line price as to what the seller's property would have sold for with or without those features after the extrapolations.

Let's say you have three comps. Each comp now has handwritten, adjusted prices circled on it of $295,500, $297,000, and $296,250 respectively. You gather the comps in front of the three of you.

Look at the comps and say, "MMJ, based on these recent comparable sales, what do you think your property will eventually sell for?"

You just closed. So what do you do? Shut up and wait for them to respond. Wait. Use it word for word. Look at the wording. Analyze it. Based on the comps that your sellers just agreed to item by item, what do they think their property will sell for? Don't ask about their *home*, which has emotional connotations. Refer to their *property*. And let them see their property stacked up against the other sold properties. What do they think it will eventually sell for?

Notice that the question carefully does not ask what you should *ask* for the property. You are simply asking, based on the comps they just ratified, what it will eventually *sell for*.

The question is a reasonable one, don't you think? You originally asked if they would like to participate in this pricing exercise. They agreed. Based on that exercise, what have they learned?

They have to say, "Well, based on those comps, it looks like our property will sell for about $297,000."

That's what most reasonable people would say.

Guess what? They have to say that. They have to say that because you cannot and will not go on until they do. If you do not get price agreement, you lose the game.

I don't mean what the asking price should be, mind you. We're simply talking about eventual sales price here. Therefore, if they say anything else, either they didn't understand the question, they don't agree with the comps, or they can't live with the price.

If they can't live with the price, you may have a financing problem, or a motivation problem. Best you get it resolved right now. Make sure they understand the question. Go over the comps again. Ask about their loan(s) again on the property. A smart lender will try to work it out with them if that's the issue.

If it's a motivational problem, the sellers may say something like, "I don't care what those comps say. I think it's worth $350,000!"

You say, "I'd love to get you $350,000. The more you get, the more I make. Isn't that right? The problem is that my buyers are going to ask to see the comps to make sure they're not overpaying for the property. These are the best comps I've got. If you've got better ones, I'd be happy to use them. Meanwhile, in this market, in this price range, nobody I know is paying over market value for properties. Why don't we try $297,000 and see what happens?"

Yes, there are unreasonable, unmotivated people out there. Let them work with another agent.

The answer you will get from a reasonable, motivated seller, if he understands the question and agrees with the comps, will be, "Well, based on those comps, it looks like it will sell for about $297,000."

You now have price agreement. You can go on.

Step #8: Write up the listing. Fill out the agreement at the market price, 6 percent commission for 180 days. Hand the sellers a pen and point at the appropriate signature line. Freeze. Don't talk. You know Rule #2: The first one to talk loses. Your seller doesn't know that rule.

Fully 50 percent of the time, the seller will simply sign.

Do you realize what this means? It means that you have just effectively doubled your listing presentation effectiveness. You were getting one in four. Now, all you did was change your presentation a little, go through six steps by the book, then get price agreement. All you had to do was fill out a form, turn it around, and hand them a pen. They just signed it. Over. Done. Nothing to it. Are you lucky, or what?

When the seller signs, put all your materials away, and go directly to step nine.

What happens if the seller doesn't sign? Can we close any of those people and take it from 50 to 75 percent or higher? You bet!

When a seller doesn't sign, it means just one thing. He has an objection. Do you know what those objections are? Do you have scripts to handle them? We'll go over that in the next chapter.

Meanwhile, if the sellers have no objections, just keep filling out all the appropriate paperwork and have them sign.

As part of this paperwork, be sure to fill out a Seller's Net Sheet. This form shows the seller the cash they will receive at closing after all expenses. If you agree to take the listing at higher than the eventual sales price you agreed on in Step #7, base your net sheet on that lower price.

Let's say, for example, that you've agreed that the eventual sales price will be $297,000, but you have agreed to list the property at $309,950. A few days later, an offer comes in. The offer price is $297,000. Now, when you present the offer, all you need to do is pull out your copy of the Seller's Net Sheet, showing the $297,000 sales price. You congratulate the sellers and encourage them to sign the contract, saying, "So we can put up a sold sign, you folks won't have to be inconvenienced any more, and you can get on with your lives!"

Step #9: Explain in detail what will happen next. Explain what will happen during the listing period and what will happen when they get an offer. Make sure the sellers understand how offers are handled. Tell them what happens during escrow, the loan approval and property inspection processes, and how the closing works. Educate them. Make them feel like they know as much as you do.

CHAPTER TEN

The Five Seller Objections

If you analyze the scripts of the game, you'll find *only five basic objections* you may face after you have price agreement, have filled out the listing agreement, and the sellers have signed it.

It is clearly to your advantage to anticipate these potential objections and have scripts prepared to answer them. You will get these objections at some point in your career. Your scripted responses to them should be so well rehearsed that (1) you will actually be excited about getting the objection, and (2) your response is so automatic, the script leaps to your tongue immediately.

You must rehearse and learn your scripts, word for word, until they are second nature. You simply cannot be thinking about what you're going to say while the game is progressing. Instead, you must be paying attention to the nuances of the play, like the sellers' physical attitude or body language, their intonation, their interrelationship, and the actual meaning of what they are saying.

It's like playing tennis. A tennis player in a tournament cannot be thinking about how to make a backhand shot. He needs to think about where he's going to hit it. The "how" must be so ingrained, it's natural. A tennis player learns through practice. The professional tennis player has hit thousands of backhand shots in practice. Have you ever seen a professional tennis player hit a cross-court backhand winner dead in the corner? It seems effortless!

How about a skier? Or a piano player? Have you ever learned a foreign language? These are all learning processes. Handling sellers' objections is just the same. The scripts provided here are proven and effective responses to such objections.

Objection #1: Price
Possible sellers' comment: *"Why don't we try $330,000 and see what happens?"*

Price is the single, number one, most important objection you will face. Remember, it's not location, location, location. It's price, price, price. You've already agreed that the property will eventually sell for $297,000. However, the seller wants to ask a higher price, reasoning that it will provide room to negotiate. There is a whole chapter ahead devoted to this one. It's called the Price/Value Relationship Dance. It's all about educating your sellers about how this business really works, and making them feel like insiders and true partners in the process.

Objection #2: Commission
Possible Sellers' Commission Objection SCRIPT #1: *"Are you guys still at 6 percent?"*

There are three major rebuttals to the commission objection. Your scripts for each are as follows:

Agent Commission Objection Response (COR) SCRIPT #1: 7 percent?

"I haven't gone to 7 percent yet. However, some of my clients have asked me to take the commission to 7 percent in this market. Do you have any idea why? You know I work on commission. You know I make no money when I take this listing. It costs me money. I only make money when the escrow closes. In this market, a buyer is a precious commodity. If I had two identical listings, one at 6 percent, the other at 7 percent, which one do you think I would sell first? Do you think I have any control at all over my buyers? Because of the market and because it is my livelihood, I will not even show a listing under 6 percent, if possible. Other agents feel the same way. It could happen that one of those agents has your perfect buyer. I'm not saying you have to go to 7 percent. I'm just telling you that some of my sellers have asked me to do so. Would you prefer 6 or 7 percent?"

Agent COR SCRIPT #2: Disincentive?

"MMJ, I understand that you want a 5 percent listing. It's natural. After all, 1 percent of $297,000 is $2,970. That's a lot of money. The problem is that it doesn't work that way. Instead of offering me an incentive to sell your property, you're offering me a disincentive. It is simply not in your best interest, especially in this market, to offer a disincentive. I'm not saying you must go to 7 percent, but please don't make me go out with less than 6 percent, which is still standard in our area."

Sellers' SCRIPT #2: "I won't pay a penny over 5 percent."

Agent COR SCRIPT #2: At full price?

"MMJ, if I go out and find you a buyer who loved your home, would be an asset to the neighborhood, and would pay you every dollar you were asking, you would pay me 6 percent wouldn't you?"

Sellers' SCRIPT: "Well, sure, at full price I would."

Agent COR SCRIPT: "That's all the listing agreement says. Look at it right here. That is all you are agreeing to. You are only obligated to pay a 6 percent commission if I bring you a full price offer or any other offer you are willing to accept."

Objection #3: Competition

Sellers' SCRIPT: "We've made an appointment for another broker to come by."

Agent Competition Response SCRIPT: "Great. I'll be glad to call and let them know the property is listed, tell them about its features, and let them know how well you've priced it. And they can still get a commission for selling it."

The sellers will be relieved. They don't want to go through another listing presentation. They think all listing presentations are like yours!

Objection #4: Motivation

Sellers' SCRIPT: "We really don't want to sell."

Check it out. If you believe them, thank them for their time, tell them about your monthly newsletter, ask if they'd like to be put on your list, and ask WDYK. If you think there's a chance to motivate them, respond like this:

Agent Motivation Response SCRIPT: "Let's see. We agree that the property is probably worth about $297,000 in today's market, right? If I were able to go out tomorrow and find a buyer who would give you $297,000 in hard, cold cash, would you be willing to take their money?"

Objection #5: Term

Sellers' SCRIPT: "What's this hundred and eighty days? I won't go a day over ninety!"

Agent Term Response SCRIPT: "In this market, all my listings are a hundred and eighty days."

Shut up. Wait for a response.

About half the time, the sellers will just agree and sign. Some sellers, however, won't budge from ninety days.

If that's the case, you say, with a flourish, "For you, ninety days."

Make the change on the listing agreement, initial it and turn it back to the sellers, pen in hand, poised over the appropriate signature lines.

Sellers' SCRIPT: "We want to think about it."

This is a stalling tactic, not an objection. Find out what the true objection is.

Ninety percent of sellers try to wriggle out of making a decision. (See Rule #3: 90 percent of the people in this world can't make a decision. Don't ask them to.) Do not repeat the whole listing presentation. Simply ask, "Why?"

Agent Stalling Response SCRIPT: "I can certainly understand your wanting to think about it, MMJ. After all, selling your house is one of the biggest investment decisions most of us make. Of course, the best time to make a decision is when you have all the facts. Obviously, you feel you need more facts. Just what facts do you need? Why don't we see if we can't take care of any questions or concerns you may have while I'm here?"

You must probe here until you get a *real* reason, other than they want to think about it. Guess what you will find the reason to be? Right. One of the five major objections listed above. However, you can't handle the objection until you get it.

"Good Guy/Bad Guy" Seller Response:

This is usually where the wife is ready to list, but the husband wants to drag his feet. The way to handle this is to divide and conquer.

Agent Good Guy/Bad Guy SCRIPT: Look at Mrs. Jones and say, "Well, Mrs. Jones, it looks like you are ready to get started this evening. Is that correct?"

She will look at her husband and say, "What do you think, George?"

At that point, you immediately break in and say with a big smile, "I didn't ask Mr. Jones, Mrs. Jones. What would *you* like to do? Would you like to get started this evening?"

She's most likely to say, "Well, yes, I would."

Look at Mr. Jones and say, "Mr. Jones, Mrs. Jones says she would like to get started this evening. What do you say? Is that all right with you as well?"

What's he going to say? He'll probably say, "Well, fine. Let's get started tonight."

CHAPTER ELEVEN

Handling Seller Price Objection: The Price/Value Relationship Dance

Price is the single, most important objection you will face from a seller in the Listing Presentation Game. Pricing the property correctly is part of the eighth step in the game. The seller's wish to overprice the property is normal, logical, extremely commonplace, and the biggest problem you will face in getting the property sold. The listing presentation confronts this problem. The key to the success of the presentation is the sequence. One step should not be taken until the prior step is completed.

In this case, the prior step was Step #7: Get Price Agreement. Once you got price agreement, you went immediately to Step #8: Write up the Listing.

As soon as your seller agreed that his property would sell for about $297,000, you completed the listing agreement with a 6 percent commission for 180 days, and got the sellers' signatures.

Half the time the seller will simply sign. What do you do when he doesn't? What do you do when he picks up the agreement, looks it over, and says:

Sellers' Price Objection SCRIPT: "Why don't we try $330,000 and see what happens?"

Agent Price Response SCRIPT: "I can certainly understand your wanting to try $330,000, MMJ. That's exactly how all my sellers feel. Heck, that's how I felt, before I learned how things really worked. I felt that you should increase the price from what you know will be the actual eventual sales price, so you can have room to negotiate. Isn't that pretty much how you feel, MMJ?"

"Yes, it is."

"MMJ, I wish I could list your property for $500,000. After all, the more I sell it for, the more I make. Isn't that true?"

Here Comes the Price/Value Relationship Dance

The purpose of the dance is to educate the seller to price his property at market, no more.

The Four Dance Steps

There are four steps to the Price/Value Relationship Dance. The dance's name refers to the principle that nothing sells unless the value appears to be greater than, or at least as great as, the price.

The first three steps can be summarized by these questions:

1. "Have you ever heard of a property being priced below market and selling in one day above market due to bidding and multiple offers?"

2. "Do you have any idea why, MMJ?"

Dance Step #1: Broker Motivation

Agent SCRIPT: "How are we real estate agents paid, MMJ? You know I don't make a dime when I take this listing, don't you? In fact, it costs me money. We make our money on commissions. We only get paid when an escrow closes. A market price listing to an agent means a sale and a closing about to happen. Agents know this and want to be the one earning that commission.

"Commissions are how they feed their families. They get excited. They call all their clients. They get their clients excited. They generate a feeling near frenzy. Fear and greed are the two great motivators.

"Conversely, how does the agent feel when he sees another overpriced listing? He yawns. Boring the agents by pricing the property over what we know it will eventually sell for really isn't in our best interests, is it, MMJ? Why don't we try $297,000 and see what happens?"

The last sentence is the scripted closing question. Use it word for word.

Remember, after you ask a closing question, shut up and wait for a response. The first one to talk loses.

Also, always remember that when they ask this question at this point in the game, they are agreeing to list with you. It's just a matter of price agreement. However, for you to win the game, the listing must be priced at market. If the sellers agree, just have them sign the listing and your other forms, and go straight to Step #9. But if they say they still want to try $320,000, go to:

Dance Step #2: Buyer Motivation

Agent SCRIPT: "Can you put yourselves in the shoes of a buyer, MMJ? Let's say you've just been transferred here from Cincinnati. Let's say you want to purchase a home in this area for around $300,000. What are you going to do?"

Sellers' SCRIPT: "Well, we'd probably find a good agent to show us all the best properties in that price range that meet our requirements."

Agent: "That's right. Let's say the agent shows you four identical homes. I mean identical in size, identical in lot, pool, bedrooms, kitchen, and so on. Let's say that three are priced at $320,000, and one is priced at $297,000. What would you think? You'd think that the one priced at $297,000 was a bargain, wouldn't you? You'd think you should act fast and offer full price, or you might lose it. In fact, wouldn't you look at the other houses and worry about insulting the seller asking $320,000 by offering less? Why don't we try $297,000 and see what happens?"

Wait for the sellers to respond. If they agree, sign them up. If they still want to try a higher price, say $310,000, go on to:

Dance Step #3: Americans Are a Non-Negotiating Culture

Agent SCRIPT: "When we go out to purchase things, how often do we negotiate the price? Usually for big-ticket items, like cars or houses, right? How often do we buy a car or a house? Not very often.

"When we go down to the grocery store to buy a loaf of bread, do we walk up to the grocer and negotiate the price? If we did, the grocer would probably think we were nuts.

"It's the same with houses, MMJ. People prefer not to negotiate. So, why don't we try $297,000 as a firm price? Why don't we try $297,000, resolving not to take one penny less? Why don't we try $297,000, and see what happens?"

Wait for the sellers to respond to your closing question. If they agree, sign them up. If they say want to try $305,000, go on to

Dance Step #4: Your Buyer Is Going to Get a Loan

Agent SCRIPT: "It's interesting to note the sellers' conception of what will happen when they sell their home. They think that somehow a buyer will appear, love the home at first sight, and write a check for $297,000.

"Actually, it's a very complex process. As part of that process, the buyer will take out a new loan on the property. Interest payments are about the only tax break left these days, aren't they? So almost surely, your buyer will want to get the maximum loan available. What that means to you is in order for your buyer to get a loan, your property has to appraise at market value.

"The lender will appraise your property in exactly the same way as we just did when we tried to determine the price your property will eventually sell for. The lender will look at the same comparable sales and extrapolate them, just as we did. Guess what price he'll come up with? That's right, about $297,000.

"Lenders are being very conservative in this market. What that means to you is that even if you were to sell the property at $305,000, the lender would probably blow your sale by refusing to appraise the property higher than market value. I can tell you from experience that buyers get very upset when they think they've been taken advantage of. Usually, they'll just walk away from the whole transaction, very bitter at the seller and the agents. So why don't we try $297,000 and see what happens?"

Agent Price Objection Response Summary

Agent SCRIPT: "I can understand your desire to ask a higher price, MMJ. As a professional real estate agent, I know all sellers feel the same way. It's logical. The problem is that it doesn't really work that way. It's my job as a professional to educate you as to how the real estate market really works, so you can use that information to your advantage. After all, what we want to do here is sell your property for the highest possible price, in the least possible time, with the least inconvenience to you, isn't that true? The way to do that is by pricing the property correctly initially. For isn't it true that it's only when value appears greater than price, or at least equal, that anything sells?

"I've never been able to understand why anyone would want to have their home on the market for any longer than necessary. It certainly is no fun. It's an inconvenience keeping it clean and picked up, ready to show at a moment's notice, with agents calling, even dropping by unannounced.

"Have you ever heard of a property that was listed below market and sold above market in one day because of multiple offers bidding the price up above the asking price? I can assure you it is happening even in today's market. Do you have any idea why?

"Pricing can generate enthusiasm or boredom. Boredom won't sell your property in this market. Real estate agents earn their living on commission. A well-priced home means a very high probability of a commission. That will get them excited. They'll get on the phone, call up all their buyers, and get them excited. Imagine all those agents out there calling all those buyers.

"Think of the fear and greed that will set in about that property. That's what sells property for more than market. Now, I'm not saying you have to price the property below market. I'm just explaining how the market works so you won't price your property over market as many sellers and agents do.

"An over-market–priced property has little or no chance of generating a commission and will not get agents' attention or interest. They'll feel that the property is a waste of their time. Just another overpriced listing. Yawn.

"The agents may show the property to some of their buyers. However, the buyers are not motivated to act on an overpriced listing. They will wait.

"Buyers and agents alike live in our culture. They are not used to having to negotiate. They think if a property is overpriced, that price is what the seller wants or has to get, to sell. They don't want to be embarrassed with an offer that may be perceived as insulting.

"And even if, by some miracle, you do sell it over market value, it won't appraise. The bank will blow the deal out of the water and you've gone through all that trouble for nothing. Why don't we try $297,000 and see what happens?"

Do you like the dance? Do you like the tune? Does the rhythm fit? Does it make sense? Is it fun?

You may want to use these scripts word for word. You may decide to change them around a little to suit your personality. That's fine. I can assure you, however, that this works. It works, word for word. It's the truth. It is professional information that is extremely beneficial to the seller. Its logic is impossible to overcome: To optimally sell a home in today's market, it must be priced at market. Period. Any reasonable person will ultimately accept this logic and will appreciate your professionalism and salesmanship.

Don't forget for a minute that sellers believe that their listing agent will sell their property. Because of that, and because they are aware of market conditions, they want—no, they demand—a professional, someone they perceive as a great salesperson.

If you do the dance successfully and get the property priced right, that's you.

CHAPTER TWELVE

The Buyer Presentation Game

Real estate agents constantly prospect for clients. We've discussed that many may not prospect enough or efficiently, but they do prospect. They take their floor time. They hold an occasional open house. They make a few phone calls. They get referrals from their friends and family.

What happens is they find people who think they want to buy a house. Often, these people are shown some property, but they don't buy immediately, not finding that perfect property. They are in a waiting mode.

Every agent has some of these people. Agents sometimes rate them. These are "A" buyers; the waiters may be "B'" or "C" buyers. Some agents have five. Some have thirty. Among the agents as a group, these buyers can be seen as a "buyer pool."

The buyer pool concept explains a lot about how the business works. It explains, for example, how a well-priced property will usually sell during the first two weeks it is on the market and why, if it doesn't, it is because it is overpriced.

What happens? The property is first exposed to the buyer pool. A property comes on the market, and the agents quickly compare its price and features to the wants and needs of their personal buyer pool. They will show the property to those whose needs it might meet. This is when the property will get its maximum exposure, when it's first exposed to the buyer pool. After that, it will only be exposed to new buyers as they come into the market, unless, of course, there is a price reduction sufficient to reintroduce it to the buyer pool.

When we advertise a property, are we really trying to sell that particular property? Not always. Typically, we're advertising that property to make the phone ring, so agents can make appointments to meet motivated buyers and sellers. When we hold a house open, are we really trying to sell that house? Not necessarily. What we're doing is prospecting for our buyer pool.

In fact, isn't that what prospecting is all about? Aren't we really trying to build up our inventory of motivated clients? Isn't that why the MLS works? The MLS allows us to expose our listings to a substantially larger buyer pool than we have on our own, or even at our office. The FSBO thinks, as many sellers do, "All he did was put it on MLS."

In a way that's true. But that works because the agents have been out working all day, finding motivated clients.

This is the very basis of Major Concept #1: Your number one job is finding motivated clients. These clients form your personal listing inventory and your personal buyer pool. It is only your effectiveness and success in finding motivated clients that you are able to take a listing, write a contract, close an escrow, or make anything happen.

Sellers need to understand this. We're advertising to develop our buyer pool. Their house will sell from our buyer pool, not from an ad in the paper. Our job as a listing agent then can be seen, not as their salesperson, but as their marketing coordinator. As marketing coordinator, it our job to make sure, first and foremost, that the property is priced correctly to maximize exposure to the buyer pool. Second, it is our job to make sure the buyer pool is quickly and effectively informed of the property and its features. Third, we must optimize the negotiations and make sure the client is properly protected contractually.

"Everybody out of the Pool!"

Now that we understand the buyer pool concept, I'll bet you're thinking that the buyer game is to increase our buyer pool. Wrong. That's the purpose of prospecting. The purpose of the buyer game is to get the prospects you do get *out of your pool!*

All buyers are not the same, particularly with regard to motivation. Remember our Major Concepts? Motivated means "has to." The best client is the motivated personal referral. What this means to us is if a buyer has to buy, we will work with that buyer differently than one who doesn't have to buy. If the buyer is a personal referral, we will work differently than we will with a cold client.

Let's divide clients into two groups: cold and warm. Warm means buyers who are transferred or otherwise have to buy. Cold means any other buyers. Cold buyers can be, for example, buyers we meet at an open house or pick up on an office floor call. Both groups go into the buyer pool. You must take both groups through the five steps of the Buyer Presentation Game.

The difference is that you will work with warm buyers until they buy. It's called "Buy or Die." However, you will only give cold buyers a limited chance.

You will take them through all the steps, give them your very best shot, but if they don't buy or list with you immediately, like a strict lifeguard, you throw them out of the pool. It's called, "Buy or get fired."

Our job is to get buyers out of the pool. The only ways out of the pool are buying or leaving. There are buyers who like being in the pool. They like looking at property with you. They will do it for months. They won't buy, and they won't leave. Do you see a problem here? These are nice people who say they want to buy. They even think they want to buy. The problem is, these people are wasting your time. They may be the only buyers you have. You don't want to fire them.

I've found that out of every three cold buyers who say they're buyers, two aren't. In order to avoid wasting two-thirds of your time working with buyers who really aren't and maximizing your chances with the one in three who really is, you need to take them all through the five steps of the Buyer Presentation Game. If they don't buy then, refer them to another agent.

You have to take them all through the five steps because there is no other way. You can't ask them, "Are you motivated?"

Well, you can ask, but it will do no good whatsoever. An unmotivated buyer will look you right in the eye and say, "You bet!"

Then they'll never buy.

Whether they are motivated or unmotivated, their actions will eventually uncover their motivation. When I say fire them or throw them out of the pool, what I really mean is let them, through their actions, prove to you they are worth spending your time, energy, gasoline, and tires on.

How can they prove it to you? Remember Major Concept #7: Motivated Buyers Are in the Market Seven Days a Week?

Are unmotivated buyers in the market seven days a week? Hardly. So what happens if you work with only one or two buyers at a time full-time, calling every day to report on your progress in finding their property? Remember Rule #6: Follow Up, Every Day. Would a motivated buyer like that? Absolutely. Would an unmotivated buyer?

On the third or fourth day in a row, you call and say, "Well, Mr. Jones, I worked on our project all day yesterday and didn't find anything. Don't be discouraged. I'll be out again all day today. I'm sure I'll find something soon. Just as soon as I do, you can run out here and tie it up. If I don't, well, I'll report in again tomorrow morning and let you know my progress. Okay?"

What's a motivated buyer going to say? He'll say, "Great!"

What's an unmotivated buyer going to say? He'll say, "Well, you know, we were talking about it last night, and you know, we really aren't that interested!"

Ah-h. He just took himself out of your pool. You can say, "As I told you, I work for my buyers full-time. There are lots of people who need and appreciate that kind of service. I should be helping those people right now. Since you're really not that interested, why don't I turn you over to one of my associates, to free me up to work with someone that really has to buy now? Would that be okay with you?"

The rules of the Buyer Presentation Game are simple. You meet the buyers and sell them a house on the same day, showing them a maximum of three.

CHAPTER THIRTEEN

Five Steps to the Buyer Presentation Game

Step #1: Appointment

Step #2: Qualify/The W-4 Gambit

Step #3: Eureka!

Step #4: Show

Step #5: Close

There are two assumptions I must make before we get into playing the game. One, you must know the paperwork. Whatever forms and contracts you use in your office must be so familiar to you, you can read and understand them upside down. You must have absolutely no fear of the paperwork. You must never be reluctant to write a contract simply because you are unfamiliar with it.

Second, you must know the inventory cold. The best way to do this is not to tour on your MLS tour day. You'll have listings of your own open. The best way to do this is to schedule four new properties a day, on your own, or with a member of your buyer pool. Plan on spending twenty to thirty minutes on each property. It's not unethical to develop rapport with the sellers. You're not soliciting their listing.

Remember, chances are the seller may be unhappy with his agent for not following up. When his house sells, he may want another agent to find them something to buy. He may need an out-of-town referral package. He may have a friend who's thinking of selling. Do not talk to him about his property, his agent, or his agent's company.

Because I like to list my properties at market value, and most properties are listed above market value, I have had agents actually ask my sellers why they priced their property so low. That's unethical. It's also stupid. It reveals to the seller the incompetence of the agent. Had I not warned the seller that this might happen in Step #9 of the Listing Presentation Game, it might have alarmed him.

Don't talk about the listed property. Don't talk about the price, the staging, the marketing, anything. You can only talk to that seller about that property if it has expired or has been canceled.

Don't talk about the other agent or his company. I make it a rule to pretend there are no other agents out there. Never ask a buyer or a seller if he is working with another agent. Never. If asked whether you know another agent by name, just answer yes or no. Make no comment, good or bad.

I really don't care about the other agent. I care about the client. The other agent is irrelevant to our dealings, unless, of course, the other agent happens to have the client's listing. I'll respect the contractual relationship between them and will in no way attempt to interfere with it. Otherwise, I simply dismiss the thought of the other agent.

Some agents say they will never work with a buyer who is working with another agent. Some agents insist on getting an exclusive authorization to purchase from a buyer. Some agents even want to get a deposit from the buyer. Why? Just follow the Five Steps. The buyer will appreciate it. You'll save a lot of time and agony.

Step #1: Appointment

Make the appointment to meet with the buyers in person. Do not try to sell on the telephone. Telephones are only for making appointments and asking questions. To sell, you must develop trust, confidence, and rapport with the buyer. This is best done in person. To sell, you must qualify the buyer. This is best done in person.

Your first appointment should be at your office. You don't know these people. There are some very strange people out there. Don't invite trouble. If the office is a huge inconvenience, then meet them at a title company office or a restaurant. Never, ever meet a prospect you don't know at a property.

You don't know them. You don't know their wants and needs. You don't know their budget. You don't know their tax situation. You don't know their likes and dislikes. The property they want to meet you at might not be at all what they are looking for. You might both just be wasting your time.

An unmotivated buyer is just curious and doesn't really care if you know his needs. It's fair to assume that, if a buyer won't make an appointment with you at your office, he isn't motivated. Let some other agent meet him at some vacant house, out in the middle of nowhere, in the middle of the night. Sorry. A motivated buyer is in the market seven days a week. He doesn't want to waste his time either. He wants you to know his wants and needs, his likes and dislikes. He'll meet you at your office.

Step #2: Qualify

The only reason you made the appointment in the first place was to qualify the buyer. You did not make the appointment to show property. After you qualify the buyer, you may find there is nothing to show. You may find that what you were planning on showing is totally out of the question for this particular buyer. It would have been a waste of time for both of you showing that property.

As in the Listing Presentation Game, you must understand there is a reason for each step and for the sequence of each step. For optimum results, you must complete each step completely and in sequence. The qualification step is crucial!

It is generally true that people don't buy things from others unless they have trust and confidence in them. In the purchase of a home, which is one of the major purchases in a person's life, this is particularly true. It is critical, then, that you build rapport with your buyers before you show them property. As we found in the Listing Presentation Game, one of the best ways to build rapport is to ask questions and take notes.

It is also generally true that you can't sell anyone anything unless you first find out what they want. "Find a need, and fill it!"

One of the best ways to do this is to ask questions and take notes.

Qualifying is about asking questions.

Agent Buyer Qualification SCRIPT:

"MMJ, I have just a few questions I'd like to ask you so that I can provide you with the very best possible service. I believe that the more I know about what you want, the better I can help you find the home of your dreams. Before I start, though, I'd like to tell you just a little about myself and my company, so you'll know with whom you are dealing."

Do that, then tell them how you work. "I work with only one or two buyers at a time. I work with them full-time. I'll look for property for you every day until I come up with what I think is your perfect house. I'll call you every day to report my progress. I've found that people who want to purchase property really appreciate that level of service. Do you think that level of service would be of any benefit to you?"

Then you ask questions. Where are they from? Where are they are going? Why? Have them describe their dream home and give you a prioritized list of its features.

Don't ask, "How much do you make?"

Instead, ask, "What is your budget for a down payment? What is your budget for monthly payment?"

Often, the buyer has been looking for some time and hasn't purchased because he has been looking in too low a price range.

The W-4 Gambit Agent Script:

"MMJ, based on your budgeted payment of $3,000 a month, a lender would say that your combined gross incomes, before taxes are withheld, but after long-term obligations, should be $7,500 (You divided $3,000 by .4). Is that about right?"

The prospect responds, "No, we make a lot more than that. Between the two of us, before taxes, we make $12,500 a month."

Agent: "Based on that figure, the lender would recommend monthly payments of $5,000 a month. With your budgeted down payment of $100,000, that would make the target price of our project $600,000."

Prospect: Gulp. "We don't want to be house poor. We were thinking (and have been looking for the last six months) more around $400,000. The $3,000 monthly payment would be much more comfortable for us."

Agent: "I can certainly understand your thinking. Most of my buyers feel the same way. At least until I explain how it really works. MMJ, have you ever wondered how we sell all these high-priced homes? It's simple, really. It's our tax laws. Home mortgage payments are just about the only write-off left to us. How much are your current house payments? If I could show you how a $5,000 payment is really only a $3,000 payment, would you be interested in looking at a $600,000 property?"

Prospect: "Look, my problem is really cash flow. I understand that I can write off my payments. However, I can't wait until the end of the year to get it."

Agent: "How many exemptions are you currently taking?"

Prospect: "Well, my wife takes one and I take none. It's a forced savings program. We like to get money back from the government every year."

Agent: "I can certainly understand that. Tell me, how much interest is Uncle Sam paying you on that? (Big smile) Seriously, it used to be true that the IRS could keep your money and not pay you any interest on it. Then, several years ago, Congress decided that was not a good deal for us citizens and declared that the IRS had to allow us only to pay what we actually owed, and not one red cent more. How they do that is with what they call exemptions. You simply put the number of exemptions on your W-4 Form. That will balance out the taxes you owe so you don't pay more monthly than necessary to break even with your actual tax obligation. Take your situation for example. Your payment of $5,000 is nearly all tax-deductible. For our purposes, let's say it all is. We figure 34 percent taxable state and federal. Thirty-four percent of $5,000 is $1,700 in tax savings a month. That means you can go down to your payroll department, legally declare the correct number of exemptions, and give yourself a $1,700 a month pay raise. The $4,000 you got back on taxes last year, divided by twelve, is $333 a month. If you were to add those exemptions, you would now be getting a pay raise of $2,033 a month. Another way to look at that $2,000 per month is that you are making $3,000 of your monthly house payment of $5,000, and Uncle Sam is making $2,000. Make sense? Now do you see why we sell all those expensive houses?"

The W-4 Gambit works. Just be sure that you have talked to an accountant and relate it to current tax laws. If there's one thing we can count on, it's changing tax laws. If you have trouble understanding this concept, talk to an accountant about it until you do. Have your clients call their payroll departments, and check it out. I had a guy really excited about this. He wasn't sure if he could believe me. After all, we had just met an hour before. He called his payroll department in Dallas. Then he really got excited. He bought a house that day.

I did this to an accountant. He looked at me and said he'd never really looked at it that way before. He bought a house that day.

Think about it. People have been looking, probably with another agent, and they're discouraged. Sometimes, they've been looking with another agent for months.

These clients really believed they wanted to buy a $400,000 home. They couldn't seem to find one they liked. They saw an for a $350,000 home that sounded great. Always in the market for a good deal, they called me.

The average agent would have given them the address. They would have driven by and eliminated not just the property, but the agent as well. The average agent might have made an appointment. He would have grabbed his MLS book and run them out to the advertised property. They would have dismissed him and the property.

Instead, I sat the buyers down and asked a bunch of questions, took notes, found a need, and filled it. I found that they hadn't considered the tax aspects of the purchase. I developed trust, confidence, and rapport by educating them about how the business really works. They rewarded me by buying from me. Not the agent they had been working with for six months. Me. That's why I don't care if they are working with another agent. That's why the fact that they are working with another agent is simply irrelevant.

Can't you imagine the excitement. It all sinks in, and the Joneses look at each other and say, "You mean we can actually afford a $600,000 home?"

I don't know about in your neighborhood, but in mine, a $600,000 home is far different than a $400,000 home.

A W-4 Gambit Sidebar: The Loan Broker

I have presented this concept to hundreds of agents. Many agents simply don't understand how to do it. That's okay. Some of the top agents in the country don't get it, either. The main thing is to understand that buyers are simply reluctant to tell real estate agents their real financial situation. Some clients are actually afraid the agent will show them something in their real price range. Their thinking seems to be that they either want the agent to find them a deal or at least keep them in their comfort level.

If you find this W-4 concept difficult, interview loan agents until you find one that understands it. Most don't. The top ones do. Top loan agents who work with top real estate agents tell me that their agents won't let anybody in the car until they've been qualified by the loan agent.

A good loan agent can help you. Find one. Interview them until you find one:

A. With whom you have personal rapport;

B. Who you believe understands finances and the W-4 concept of getting buyers up to the proper price range;

C. Who can tell you immediately if a buyer simply won't qualify, and;

D. Who will follow up.

As a rule, this loan agent will work for a loan broker, not for a direct lender—a bank or savings and loan. Direct lenders are in and out of the market. Most loan brokers have dozens—the large ones have hundreds—of lenders to choose from and can always find the best rates among them. They're not locked in to a particular lender who can raise rates and tighten qualifying ratios (and blow your deal) overnight.

Step #3: Eureka!

You made the appointment. You brought the prospects into your office where you sat down to ask questions. You found out what they were looking for. You found out what their budget was and correctly determined for yourself the price range in which they should be looking. You developed trust, confidence, and rapport. You educated them. They think you are a professional. You are now ready to take the next step. You are ready to go for the show. You are now finally ready to take them out on the street and show property. Guess what? You've decided not to show them the $350,000 house they called in on.

Eureka! Agent SCRIPT:

"Well, MMJ, based on our financial analysis of tax considerations, let's review the qualities you are looking for in your dream home."

As they talk about what they want, a picture of the very home they are describing pops into your consciousness. You just listed it yesterday. You get excited.

You say with great enthusiasm, "I've got it. I've got the perfect house. It just popped into my mind as we were going over your list. It's perfect. Would you like to see it? Right now?"

Would they ever!

"Tell us about it," they reply.

"Nope. I'll let you discover it on your own."

Buyers tend to be skeptical. They just seem to want to see for themselves and come to their own conclusions. Therefore, I don't tell them the good things about a listing, just the bad. If I tell them it has a fantastic view, chances are, they won't agree with me. When they discover it on their own, they'll be excited. Excitement is good. Emotion sells houses.

However, I do tell them about the bad things. If the house is a little dirty, I exaggerate a little. I tell them it's filthy. Dust balls. Cobwebs. Crayon marks. Grease. They get to the property, look at it, and see the dust balls, cobwebs, crayon marks, and grease. Know what they say? "Oh, it's not so bad!"

Step #4: Show

A properly qualified client should only be shown two or three properties, transferees excepted. If the client doesn't write a contract, either you have erred in qualifying or the client is not motivated. The unmotivated client should be immediately referred to an agent who is not as busy as you are.

Think about it this way. Let's say you know the inventory, cold. You know every house on the market and most that are about to come on the market. And, let's say, through proper questioning, listening, and cooperation from the clients in answering and understanding the financial and tax ramifications, you are able to qualify them to the dollar they should be spending, and the exact location, size, and amenities of the home they are seeking.

If you knew every house available and exactly the home and price they should be buying, let me ask you, how many homes are out there that meet those requirements? Only one or two.

That's why "Eureka!" works. It's a real feeling. It's difficult to find the perfect property. It's difficult to really qualify a person. It takes a real pro to know everything on the market. Those two things are difficult enough by themselves. Together, at the same time and place, is close to a miracle!

Miracles Can Happen

Let's return to MMJ. You've called the sellers to make the appointment. You told them that you might have found their buyers. You ask them to turn on all the lights, put a fire in the fireplace, and turn on some soft music. They might even warm up some apple cider on the range and put some bread in the oven. You asked them to leave the house. You have asked them not to return as long as your car is parked out front.

MMJ leave the office with you in your car. You don't say anything. They are excited, full of anticipation. Anything you say is likely to spoil the mood. You drive to the home using the most attractive route. You may point out recent homes you have sold in the neighborhood. You park across the street, never uphill, from the property. With a sweeping gesture you say, "MMJ, your next home!"

You leave the car and walk slowly toward the house. You do not speak. You might point at features they may miss.

Upon entering the home, you say, "Why don't I let you explore on your own. I'll just make myself comfortable in this beautiful living room."

They go through the home two or three times. Mentally, they place their furniture. They come back to the living room trembling with excitement. You say something emotional like, "Can you imagine what it is like on that back patio on a warm summer evening with all the lights twinkling down in the valley?" Heat!

Step #5: Close

Only 10 percent of the people you show can make a decision. These people will tell you to write it up.

Ninety percent of the people you show cannot make a decision (see Rule #3). These people will not tell you to write it up. These people will always say, one way or another, "We want to think about it!"

Since the 10 percent person is going to tell you to write it up, and the 90 percent person is simply going to want to think about it, *never* ask for a decision!

Homes are purchased on emotion. They are sold on logic. Take your sellers to the kitchen table and talk business. Take your buyers into the living room, turn on some soft music, sit by the fire in a cozy chair, and talk romance. This is wooing, folks!

The emotional experience of purchasing a home is called heat. The closer to the heat, the easier the close. The closest, hottest heat is while you are inside the home. Conversely, the further from the heat, in both time and distance, the colder the client gets. The colder the client gets, the harder the close.

A properly qualified, motivated client will give you buying signals while being shown the house. Mentally placing their furniture in the property is a buying signal. Other such signals include questions like, "Does the refrigerator come with the house?"

> The answer is never yes or no.

> The answer is not, "I don't know."

> The answer is not, "Let's include it in our offer."

> The answer always is, "Did you want the refrigerator to come with the house?"

Trial Close on Buying Signals

Remember, there is a 90 percent chance that the clients will want to think about it. After all, this is one of the biggest decisions they'll ever make in their entire lives.

Just because it's a big decision doesn't mean that the buyer should hesitate. It has been my personal experience that whenever I find a property that's perfect for me, somebody else will think it's perfect for him or her too. I have lost properties when I didn't even hesitate. Hesitation just makes matters worse!

Take MMJ, for example. If they are decision makers, those 10 percent of the folks out there who can make a decision, what will they do after walking back into the living room all excited? What will a decision maker say to me at that moment? He'll say, "Write it up!"

No problem. No trial close. No close. Just write it up!

I had a referral client. He was a young man in a hurry. He was thirty-six years old, a self-made multi-millionaire. He wanted a nice house. Price was no issue. I showed him every mansion on the market. He was courteous, but decisive. Nope. Nope. Nope.

I wracked my brain. Then I recalled a story about a particular mansion that had been on the market a couple of years back. It never sold. It had 11,000 square feet just in the main house. Incredible. I tried to find out if it was still for sale. No luck. In desperation, I drove past the huge, gated entry, walked up to the mammoth front doors, and rang the bell. The owner answered. He explained that, yes, the property was for sale and in fact was listed with an out-of-the-area broker. He showed me the place. It took an hour.

I called my client. "I found your house!" I said.

"I'll be right out," he answered.

Motivated buyers are in the market seven days a week. He asked me to drive his Rolls. I didn't tell him about the property. He didn't ask. I drove up to the entry gates, and we looked down on the mansion. He said, "Write it up!"

I said, "Don't you want to see it first?"

"Nope. Here's a check. Give me a contract. I'll sign it in blank. You fill it out, all cash, full price, and thirty-day close. Call me when you get the acceptance."

That's a decision maker. Problem is, most people aren't!

Take MMJ. As a typical, normal 90 percent type, when they show up in the living room, they don't say anything about buying, even though they're obviously excited.

Don't say, "Do you want to buy this house?"

They're likely to get the nervous shakes and say, "We want to think about it."

The Trial Close Agent SCRIPT: "MMJ, would you like to see what the financing looks like on this property?"

Would they? Sure, anything to keep their minds off the magnitude of this decision.

While they were going through the house, you were preparing a little financing sheet showing that, with their down payment and the current financing rates, this home purchase would be just like that scenario you described in the office.

Now, the buyers can say to you, "Well, you were right. What a genius. Thanks for being so professional. Thanks for qualifying us and getting us to the correct price. After all, we have been looking for six months with another agent and have been terribly disappointed. And, thanks for knowing about this property. You were right. It's perfect. Thanks for letting us have the fun of discovering it on our own. It's terrific. You are terrific. Where do we sign?"

They could say this. Guess what? They won't. They are scared!

Here we are. Qualified, "Eureka'd," and shown. We have some very excited, emotional people on our hands. They've asked all the right questions. They've mentally placed their furniture. You have trial-closed on financing. It appears that everything is just like you described it back at the office. They are in the living room on a soft chair, in front of a warm fire, soft music in the background. It doesn't get any hotter than this. Don't ruin it for them. Don't ask for a decision!

The Close Agent SCRIPT: You have a contract already on the coffee table. You lean over it, pen poised in your hand, look straight at them, and ask that immortal question, "What is today's date?"

Really. That's it.

You just closed. Now, what do you do? You wait for a response. What's their script? Think, now. What would you say if I asked you what today's date is? Right. You'd say, just like they will say, "Well, let's see. Today's date is ____."

Most people will simply tell you what the date is. What's happening here is they are thinking about something other than this big decision. You go on, "The normal deposit amount on a property like this is either $5,000 or $6,000. Which would you prefer?"

You continue, "As we discussed when we went over the financing, the asking price is $600,000. It is a fair asking price. Why don't we try $600,000 and see what happens?"

About half the time, the clients will simply let you fill out the agreement, you turn it around and point to the appropriate spots, and they will sign. Sometimes they will want to discuss the price and see comps. Sometimes they will want to discuss financing options. Sometimes, they may have a property to sell first and will want to understand how a contingent offer works. Here, you never asked for a decision. You made it easier to sign than not to sign.

"Think about It" SCRIPT #1:

The other half of the time, they will say, "Wait a minute. We need to think about this."

We can certainly understand that, can't we?

That's when you say, "Isn't it true that the best time to make a decision is when we have all the facts? Well, that's just what we're doing. This agreement sets down all the facts. When we have it completed, we have all the facts right in front of us."

You then simply rephrase the last question you asked, "If you were to purchase this property, would you prefer a $5,000 or a $6,000 deposit?"

Go on that way with, "If you were to purchase this property, would you want to try $600,000 and see what happens?"

The client may be even more insistent. "We always think things through over-night before making a big decision. We will not sign an agreement today!"

That's fine. When you have the agreement finished, they will have all the facts in front of them to think over, won't they? Yes, they will.

When you finish writing the agreement, turn it around, point to the signature lines, and say, "Why don't you let me take this to the sellers tonight and see if I can get them to agree to your terms?"

Remember, this is their new home. They love it. They are excited. Fear and greed have set in. They have been looking for six months!

About half the time, they'll sign and say, "Oh, okay. Give it a try."

"Think about It" SCRIPT #2:

The other half of the time, they'll say, "We told you we are going to have to think about this overnight. We'll just take this contract home with us and get back to you in the morning."

You say, "Of course, I understand. You may certainly do that. However, before you do, let me help you by answering any questions you may have now. Obviously, if the best time to make a decision is when you have all the facts, you must feel you don't have all the facts. Since I'm here with you right now, why don't we see what facts we need."

"Well, we really have all the facts we need right now. We just need time to think it over."

Agent SCRIPT: Tell a Personal Story

"It's good to be cautious when you are making a decision, especially one of this magnitude, MMJ. In real estate, however, you must be careful of overcaution. Hesitation can cost you this house. I can tell you that I sure kicked myself for being a little hesitant on the purchase of a home that my wife and I loved.

"You see, we weren't the only ones who loved that house. In our case, our hesitation wasn't that we needed to think about whether we wanted or could afford the home. It was that we hesitated about paying the fair market price. The home had been on the market for some time. I thought that we could wing in a low offer and they might take it. The listing broker thought so as well. At least that's what he told us.

"Problem was, as soon as we signed the offer, he told the agents in his office that he had an offer, they called all their clients, and one of them wrote a full price offer on the spot. Of course, the other person got the home. We couldn't find one to replace it. To tell you the truth, I don't think my wife has ever quite forgiven me for that. Now, I'm not here to tell you my problems in life. I'm just trying to make a point."

Agent SCRIPT: Summarize and Forecast Downside

"Think about what has just happened. We met. We discussed your situation, your wants and needs, and I got lucky. You got lucky. I had just the right house. How often do you think that happens? Do you think that there's a possibility that, if you wait to think about this overnight, someone else might buy the property before you come back to me? Is that possible? Of course, it's possible.

"Then what? Can I pull this miracle off again? Can I conjure up another perfect house for you tomorrow? You know what else? You'll be mad at me. Do you know how I make 90 percent of my income? Referrals.

"My livelihood is primarily from referrals from happy clients. I'm not asking you to let me take this to the seller tonight so I can get a sale and a big commission. I really don't care about the commission. I care about my clients. I care about referrals in the future. If I let you take this paperwork home with you this evening without telling you all this, I am not doing my job for you. You may ultimately wind up angry with me and send me no referrals. That's not good business."

Agent SCRIPT: The Offer Is Contingent!

"This offer is for a sixty-day close. It's subject to your inspections. It's subject to obtaining financing. It's subject to your approval of the sellers' written disclosure statement and your unrestricted right to back out of this agreement within three days. You will have plenty of time to think this over. Just don't let someone else make the decision for you. Don't let someone else come in and tie up the property. You tie up the property first. Then think about it. What do you say, MMJ, let me take this to the seller tonight and see what he says!"

Is it in their best interest to tie the property up today? Is it true that the contingencies in the contract give them ample opportunity to think over their decision? Is it true that my business is mostly referral and I want my clients to recommend me to others because I did a good job for them? Am I trying to arm wrestle them into a bad deal here? Is it possible that another offer could come in tonight and that I could not ever find as good a property to replace it?

People Justify Their Decisions

Do they really want to think about it? They sure do. It's natural. It's normal. It's also a terrific way to lose your dream house. Don't let them. People tend to justify their decisions. If they don't sign that offer, what will they be thinking to themselves that evening? They will be justifying that decision.

They will be saying things like, "It's a good thing we didn't sign. It's too much money. We only should be buying a $400,000 house. Uncle Charlie should see it first (you know, Uncle Charlie the real estate broker from over in the next county?). We should talk to our CPA and our attorney (you know, the attorney that thinks the property is worth about half of what the sellers are asking?)."

However, should they sign the offer, what will they be thinking to themselves that evening? "I hope he gets it for us. Boy, were we lucky to run into that guy today!"

Of course, they were!

A Last Thought about Closing the Buyer

Just one last thought. Remember the very first house I sold? I went to the open house to break the listing agent for lunch. There were buyers in the house writing up an offer with a real estate agent. I had clients come by. They saw the people writing the offer. My clients wanted to buy the house. They wrote an offer. I presented the offer that night with the listing agent, who as you can imagine, was not a very happy camper. That was some expensive lunch.

During the presentation, he told the sellers that another couple had come by the open house and written an offer with another agent. "So, where's their offer?" asked the seller.

"They wanted to think about it overnight," said the agent.

"A bird in the hand," said the seller, with a big smile, as he signed my offer.

What do you suppose happened to the first people who wrote an offer? Do you think they might have been a little upset the next day to find the house had literally been sold out from under them? Do you think they might have been a little upset with their agent? Unreasonable? Maybe. Irrational? Perhaps. Real world, though.

Imagine how it might have been. These clients may have been working with this poor agent for six months. He may have shown them dozens of houses. He may have previewed dozens others. He had made a huge investment in his time, energy, gasoline, and tires. His clients finally wrote an offer. They decided to think about it overnight. Then some guy, brand new in the business, sold it to some other people that very night. Can you imagine? What luck. What a rotten business. When his clients learned they lost the house, they fired him.

You are a pro, a superstar. You know your inventory, cold. You know how to make an appointment. You know how to qualify. Because you know the inventory and how to qualify, you are often able to miraculously think of a house that's perfect for these clients. Because you are a superstar, these people believe you. They believe you know what you're doing. You do!

Sure, you know about how to show, trial close, and close. Yes, it *is* important that you operate in their best interest by not letting them do the normal "think about it" routine. Just, please remember, none of this would have happened if you hadn't met them face to face in your office before you showed them a single property and *qualified* them. Never forget, 90 percent of the close is in the qualification.

CHAPTER FOURTEEN

Negotiating and Presenting the Offer

You've found a motivated client. You've played the Listing Presentation Game or the Buyer Presentation Game and won. But you're not through yet.

There's still one major hurdle between writing a contract and a commission check. You now must get a ratified contract between a buyer and a seller that will close escrow.

We can all agree that getting a ratified contract is not difficult if the contract is written at full price, for all cash, and with the closing time the seller is looking for.

If getting a full price offer makes getting a ratified contract easier, then it appears logical that our first objective in successfully negotiating and presenting offers is to write or get full-price offers.

Getting Full-Price Offers on Your Listings

The Listing Presentation Game is structured with one major purpose in mind: getting the listing in one presentation *at market value*.

Remember all the educating we had to do to help the seller understand how the market really works? Remember that most listings are taken over market value; it is natural for the seller to want to price his home over market to have room to negotiate.

Remember the concept of a property priced under market and sold over market in one day because of multiple offers? Remember the Price/Value Relationship Dance, where we gave four clear, strong, logical reasons why pricing a property over market will actually harm its chances of selling? We used those examples to counsel our sellers that it is in their best interest not to negotiate.

Negotiation Rule #1: The best way to negotiate is to put yourself in a position where you don't have to negotiate.

Look at it this way. Say you have a high-demand property worth $100,000 in today's market. Let's say you have only two choices in offering it for sale. You can offer it at $105,000 or you can offer it at $95,000. That's it. No other choices. Now, let me ask you, under which pricing are you liable to get the highest possible price, in the least time, with the least inconvenience?

Remember, we're not talking about widgets or refrigerators here. People usually won't pay more than what you are asking for a widget. We're talking about property. Property is unique. There's only one. There is a commission driven substructure that motivates its salespeople. Therefore, there is a greater fear of loss in property, perhaps, than in other commodities. Since fear and greed are the greatest motivators, a good deal in property is a tremendous motivator to an agent or a motivated buyer. Agents properly motivated by price will generate a frenzy, resulting in multiple offers and bidding on a property. That can actually result in a sale over market value. Frenzy, multiple offers, and bidding will never occur on an overpriced property.

Of course, in a way, we are also talking about widgets. Pricing is paramount in any product. Market researchers spend millions of man-hours a year trying to determine the optimum selling price for a product. Look at DVDs. When they first came out, priced at $1,000, sales were lackluster. At $99, DVDs now sit in millions of people's homes. A computer doesn't sell at $2,000. Slap a price tag of $699 on it, and people buy!

Pricing Is Critical. You Must Know What Market Value Is.

Pricing is critical. You, as a real estate agent, must know the market well enough to accurately predetermine the eventual sales price of a property.

I have had agents tell me they can't accurately price properties in their market because the properties in their market are so different. If I didn't hear that so often, I would think that there just might be some truth to it. But I know better. It's lazy, incompetent, unprofessional Mr. Average Agent talk. I didn't say it was easy. In some markets, it clearly isn't easy.

It is a whole lot easier to establish an eventual sales price on a property in a subdivision of five hundred homes and four floor plans, with eighty sales in the last twelve months, than it is in a mixed area of homes where the price can vary by $1,000,000, and only four homes have sold in the last year.

What happens when a property sells, and the buyer goes down to his friendly lender for a loan on it? Right. The lender will send out an appraiser. Will the appraiser call back the bank and say, "I'm sorry; it's impossible?"

No. He'll do the appraisal. He'll do it based on the best comps he can find, even if he has to go miles for one. He'll come up with a price. How much is the appraiser being paid? Probably around $400. I don't get it. Why is it possible for an appraiser to do something for $400 that you can't do for $6,000? Just remember that, unless you are an appraiser, you can't call it an appraisal. It's a market evaluation. And you must do it to optimally represent the seller. You must price the property at market value. To do that, you must know market value. Then, you must educate the seller as to the value of pricing it at market value. The best way to negotiate is to put yourself in a position where you don't have to negotiate. Price the property to get full-price offers.

If It Hasn't Sold, It's Either the Agent or the Price

Is it possible you can price the property at market, and it won't sell? No. You were just wrong about market value.

Agents tell me all the time, "I've got this property priced extremely well, and it hasn't sold!"

I guess they're trying to tell me that they've heard me go on and on about this price thing, they have their property priced right, it's not selling, and I'm wrong. Guess what? I haven't got a thing to do with it. I didn't price the property. They did. All I can tell you is, if it isn't selling, it has to be either the agent or the price.

I've seen agents fail to properly manage the sale of a property so badly that I was actually able to take an expired listing and sell it for more than the other agent was asking. It's rare. Unfortunately, it happens.

Once, I took an out-of-my-area vacation property's equity as commission on a large listing. Some years later, I needed to sell it. I had never seen it. I called the broker who handled the sale for me years before and told him to price it, list it, and sell it. He mailed me a listing for $65,000. I signed it and sent it back. A month later, I hadn't heard from this agent (sound familiar?), so I called him. "What's happening?"

"Nothing. Business is terrible."

"Okay. Get back to me." He didn't.

A couple of months later, the listing was due to expire, and I received a cold mailing from another agent in the area. He was mailing to all the absentee owners in his area. I was one. I called him and explained the situation. He called me back and said he had done a market evaluation on the property, and he had some good news for me. The property was worth about $85,000. Wow. How could that be? He explained that the other agent had never put up a sign or put it on the local MLS.

The new agent sold it in a week for $82,500. Not a bad example of the potential damage our good friend, Mr. Average Agent can do, is it? Was the first agent stupid, lazy, greedy, incompetent, unprofessional, or all of the above? Mysteries!

Based on that experience and others, when an agent comes to me and tells me that his listing is priced right but isn't selling, you can understand my reaction. There is a very high probability that he or she is an Average Agent. It's almost the only logical conclusion. The only other is that they are wrong.

It is possible to err. It is possible to price a property too high, even with all good intentions of pricing it at market. Appraisers sometimes make mistakes. So can a good agent. What if, for example, we used a comp that had a seller kickback that was undisclosed? What if there was no down payment and 0 percent financing we were unaware of? Would that affect the sales price? What if the estimate of value was dead right, but the market suddenly plunged? Would that affect our eventual sales price?

Of course, all of those scenarios would affect our eventual sales price. If that's true, what's the answer to that problem? Simple. Reduce the asking price to the real market value.

Major Concept #9: You Are Not Responsible for the Market, Just for Knowing It

One of sellers' favorite scripts is, "If you just advertised it more, if you just held it open more, if you just represented me better, the property would sell."

What the seller means by that, of course, is it's your fault the property isn't selling for more than it's worth. Lots of agents fall for this one because they feel guilty, and they feel responsible. They are only responsible for knowing the market and educating their sellers about how best to sell their property in this market. Period.

Call up your stockbroker. You've got some stock that you paid $50 a share for. Tell him to sell it for $50. You just want to break even and pay the commissions out of your own pocket. That's the amount you need. He punches up the quote on your stock on his Quotron and sees that the current price is $25. What's he going to do? Is he going to put a bid offer into the stock exchange at $50? Maybe if he ran a big enough ad in the *Wall Street Journal*, he could sell it for $50?

Maybe if he set up a stand in the financial district, he could sell it on the street to some fool for $50?

Does he feel guilty? Not my stockbroker. Hey, you lay down your money and you take your chances.

You say, "You told me it was going to double!"

He says, "Not today, pal. You want out today? I'll get you $25, maybe, if the market doesn't crash first!"

"But I need that $50. I'm even willing to pay the commissions out of my own pocket!"

After he pulls himself off the floor from laughing, he says, "Look, I'm sorry. The market went against us. Nothing we can do but sell now and take our lumps, or wait it out and hope and pray that it does finally recover enough to get your money out."

Of course, he's right. You made the investment, not him. Nobody broke your arm to lay down your hard-earned money. You thought you could make some money on an investment. You were wrong. It happens all the time.

Why, then, is it that real estate agents feel responsible for their market? Why is it we feel obligated to get the seller the price he wants?

How come when we have gone to all the trouble to put together a market analysis, which sometimes can be very difficult, our work is irrelevant? "Doesn't matter, if I don't get this price, I don't (can't, won't) sell," some sellers say.

Can't you just hear a real estate agent responding to that by saying, "Not today, pal. If you want out today, it's $297,000!"

Major Concept #10: You Are Not a Principal. You are the Agent to the Principals.

One of the main differences here, between our stockbroker and our real estate situations, is that the real estate seller thinks he is negotiating with *you*. That's his first mistake. Moreover, Mr. Average Agent goes along with it.

The seller thinks he is negotiating with you because there is an underlying sentiment about this industry that says we don't really know the price, and prices are negotiable. Therefore, the best negotiator wins. Therefore, sellers come out negotiating from the very beginning. They begin with their own agents. They set up an adversarial situation from the beginning. Maybe they heard about my vacation property deal and have a right to be adversarial?

I've heard agents complain that, "The seller had five different agents, I told him the market price, but he gave it to the agent who gave him the highest market price."

Is that a good deal for the seller? Is that in his best interest? It certainly is if the highest agent was right. But the typical situation is that the high agent purposely prices the property 20 percent over market in the hopes of looking good to the seller. He hopes to get the listing, with the thought in mind that he'll eventually get the price down enough to sell it.

That might work in getting the listing. However, what good does it do anybody? That's like my stockbroker telling me he'd get me $50 for my $25 stock. That's not going to happen. I'll ask the agent who lost the listing if he went over a CMA in detail with the seller.

He'll say he did.

I ask, "Then what did the seller have to say about that?"

"Well, he said he had to get that much for his property."

That's why I emphasize harmony in the Listing Presentation Game. We must have harmony to have price agreement. In order to get price agreement we must educate the seller and make him an insider. We are working together on this project. It is the seller and me against the world.

Always Follow Up

Remember Rule #6: Follow Up. Mr. Average Agent took that listing at 20 percent over market value. He thought he could eventually beat the seller down until it sold. Problem is, he never calls the seller back. If he does, the seller does the beating. After all, this is the agent's price. Now he has to eat it. He doesn't follow up!

However, you do. You call your sellers every day to report on what's going on in the market today and to find out how many showings occurred. If you erred and priced the house too high, and you don't call every day, you will have a much more difficult time reducing it than if you do call every day.

Believe me, motivated sellers appreciate this service. A seller is in line at the grocery store. She starts chatting with her neighbor, who also happens to have her house on the market. "How are things going at your house on your sale?" she asks.

"Not so good," the neighbor admits. "You know, we never hear from our agent, and we are so upset. How are things going with your sale?"

"Well, we haven't sold yet, but we know exactly what's going on because we hear from our agent every day!"

"Every day?"

"Yes, every day. We really appreciate it!"

"What's that agent's name?"

It is possible to err. Make the sellers a true part of your team. You need to analyze the situation with them. Keep them informed. Research to find out where you may have been off. Go over that with the seller. This is not adversarial. We are pulling together.

If you're talking to them every day, making them part of the team, and keeping them informed, what are they going to say? Are they going to demand you run a half-page ad? On the other hand, are they going to suggest a price reduction?

Don't Give Your House Away, Please

Another one of my favorite seller scripts is, "I don't want to give my house away!"

For years, that one had me baffled. I'd look at sellers in shock and say something clever like, "I can certainly understand that!"

However, I really didn't understand it. I felt like saying, "Really? Everybody else does. What's your problem?"

Or, "Really? If you change your mind, give me a call, I know a good charity: me!"

Or, "Hey. You don't have to give it away. I've got $20 here in my pocket. I'll take it off your hands!"

What this turns out to be is seller negotiation with the agent. Again. The seller is saying that he knows more about the value of the property than you do. He's saying the property has some mysterious, intrinsic value that you simply don't appreciate. Actually, he's really saying that it has an intrinsic value that you are too stupid to appreciate.

How's that for a communication problem? How's that for harmony? Kind of gets you off on the wrong foot, doesn't it? Believe it or not, one seller sent nasty letters to my broker because I refused to take his listing at 20 percent over market value. Despite my best efforts to educate this particular seller as to values and how the market really works, he insisted that he was right and I was wrong.

I've been wrong before. I'll probably be wrong again, but probably not by 20 percent. I'm an independent contractor. I may decide to decline any listing I choose, for whatever reason I want. If he wants to list it for 20 percent over market and tell me I'm stupid for wanting to give his house away, I think maybe he needs another agent. Plenty of agents out there would love to take the listing. What's the big deal?

The big deal is the house never sold. And I can assure you of this; at 20 percent over market, it never will.

Ugly Duckling Becomes a Swan

Believe me, you don't ever have to give a house away to sell it. I have taken listings over market, as has every agent. It is so depressing when the agents and clients come through and sneer. It hurts. You feel like it will never sell at any price. Maybe, this one, we will have to give away. However, take the price down a little to market value, and the ugly duckling becomes a beautiful swan. Everyone loves it. Then, it sells!

What do you do when you have taken a listing at a little over market to have room to negotiate?

It is clear that it is in the sellers' best interest to take the listing at market and not negotiate, or negotiate only the fine points. You now have all the ammunition you need to do that. It's not easy. The seller's natural, logical thinking will work against you from the beginning. He will see you as a principal with whom he needs to negotiate. He thinks he needs to have room in the pricing to negotiate. He may even have the wrong idea as to the real market value of the property.

You will wind up, from time to time, losing the game, but you can still win the war. You like these people enough and they are motivated enough that you finally agree to take the listing a little high. You are still clear as to your opinion, and you've made sure of that by putting it on a Seller's Net Sheet.

You go ahead and do all the things you normally do. Especially, follow up every day. If you haven't taken it too far over market, you may get an offer. If the offer is at the net sheet figure, see that they take it and run, as we discussed before. If it is your buyer, this should be no problem. I just tell the buyer, "This is what they are asking. Here are the comps we used to determine the sales price. You decide what offer you want to make."

"Well, based on those comps, it looks like the property is worth about $297,000."

"Great. Why don't we try $297,000 and see what happens?"

Buyer Price Negotiation #1

The wrinkle here is we left ourselves open for negotiation, didn't we? We didn't apply Negotiation Rule #1. So what happens is the buyer says, "Why don't we try $267,000 and see what happens?"

Now you are forced to say, "I'm happy to take any offer you want to this seller. I'm sure he will appreciate your interest. Problem is, you and I are sitting here looking at the same comps he looked at when I listed the property. Four properties like this have sold for considerably more than that recently. I'm sure he will either counter or reject the offer. I'm just the agent here, and it's not my job to accept or reject any offer. It's my job to get the transaction together where everybody is happy. It has been my experience that it is not in the buyer's best interest to submit a below market offer. Not if the buyer wants to continue to negotiate. Not if he is willing to take the chance that the seller will become upset, reject the offer out of hand, and be unwilling or at least reluctant to deal with him further. Why don't we try $296,500 and see what happens?"

"Why don't we try $282,000 and see what happens?"

Now he's negotiating with me. This is the "split the difference offer," working from $297,000 to his first idea of $267,000.

"I'm just the agent here, Mr. & Mrs. Smith (MMS). I want you to get the very best buy on this property possible. It would be great if I could sell it to you for $282,000. However, it's not up to me. It's up to the seller. He is asking $307,000. Based on these comps, which you have both seen, it looks like it might appraise out at $297,000. Give me a chance to see if I can't get you a market deal on this property at $296,000."

The buyer says, "Why don't we try $287,000 and see what happens?"

You discuss it some more, but the buyer is firm at $287,000.

You write it up. You call the seller. Rule #1: The telephone is only for making appointments. Unless the seller is out of town, do not present the offer on the phone. You'll say you have an offer on the property and need to come over to present it. He'll ask about the offer. Don't tell him on the phone. Just say, "I'll go over the whole thing with you in a few minutes. I'll be right over."

Seller Price Negotiation #1

You go into the sellers' home. Mr. and Mrs. Jones (MMJ) are excited. They look at you expectantly. If you had a full price offer, or even one at the $297,000 you agreed would be the eventual sales price, you would have a sold sign under your arm and warmly congratulate them.

Problem is, you don't. You take them back to the kitchen table. They say, "How much did you get?"

You say, "I didn't get you what you are asking. However, I think we have something here we can work with. Remember I told you that when you got an offer, you would have a chance to look it over and then decide whether you wanted to accept it, reject it, or counter it. Tonight you will have all those choices. First, though, let me tell you a little bit about the buyers."

After you do that, you go through the offer. When you get to the price, they say, "No way we're selling for $287,000. Forget it!"

You say, "I understand the price difference. Let's go through the whole agreement and see if there are any other problems."

Isolate the objections. Get them off the price for now, and look at everything else.

"The refrigerator, too? No way."

Make notes on all the objections to the agreement.

When you have finished isolating all the objections other than price, go back to price. Bring out the comps you used. Bring out the Seller's Net Sheet. "MMJ, I know this isn't the price we discussed. I'm not recommending that you accept this price. I wrote this offer and decided to present it to you tonight because the buyers are good people, and although the offer is low, the offer keeps them from making offers on other properties while you consider this one. Do you understand?"

"The buyers have had the opportunity to review these comps, just as we have. As you can see, there are three good comps that when adjusted for our property's amenities, comp out at an adjusted price of $295,500, $296,250, and $297,000 respectively. You will recall my recommendation that we price your property at the top of that range and not negotiate an offer. My thinking was that the low offering price, in relation to other offering prices, would make us appear low and generate a full price offer. Instead, we agreed to offer the property at $307,000 in order to have room to negotiate. As you now see, we're being forced to negotiate. I'm not recommending that you accept this offer, although you are free to do so if you wish. Do you wish to accept this offer at this price?"

"No!"

"What I am recommending is that we not simply reject it, but counter it. A normal process would be the buyer and seller countering back and forth, each splitting the difference until we are each near the top and the bottom of the range. We can go through that process, too, MMJ. Or, we can look at these numbers, just like the buyer will, and reasonably determine right now, that if the property sells, it will sell somewhere between $295,500 and $297,000. Is that about how you see it, MMJ?"

"Yes."

"If that is true, why don't we figure out where we'd like to be and work out a plan to get us there? I know you'd like to be at the $307,000 you are asking, MMJ. That doesn't appear to be in the cards. Here we have some very good buyers. They know the numbers. They won't pay over the upper range for the property. However, I think I can get them up to the lower range of $295,500. Now, had we been given an offer tonight of $295,500 sitting right here in front of us, we would have to take that offer very seriously, wouldn't we? We might even choose not to counter, realizing that often our first offer is our best. In addition, we know that in this market, buyers are walking away for $1,000. With that in mind, I suggest you give me a counter offer of $297,000, with the understanding that anything I can get you over the $295,500 is 'found money,' like money you found on the street."

Buyer Price Negotiation #2

You call your buyers. You get back together with them immediately, with the counter of $297,000. You tell them, "I've worked on these sellers for two hours. This is what I finally got them to come down to. They wanted to split the difference with you; afraid you would want to negotiate, on and on. I assured them that you were fair people and did not want to take advantage of them. As you can see from the comps, $297,000 is a fair price. To be honest with you, that is the price I suggested as an asking price. I felt at that price we would get so much activity that we might even get multiple offers and bid it up even to a higher price. It didn't work out that way. However, I have to ask you, MMS, had there been other offers, you would have been thrilled to get it at $297,000, wouldn't you? Who knows, if we wait, maybe other offers will come in. How would you like to respond to this counter? You are free to accept it, counter it back, or reject it. If you accept it, I will immediately deliver it to the sellers, and you will have bought yourselves your next home. It's all over. If you counter it, I will see if I can present it tonight. They will have to decide to accept, reject, or counter again or maybe just sit on it for a while to see if any other offers come in. Of course, as long as they sit on it, you have the right to terminate the counter offer at any time before they accept it. Then we can go back out and see if we can't find you another house."

A very high percentage of buyers will simply sign the counter offer when approached like this. Your sellers just found $1,500 in the street.

Some simply won't sign the counter. Some like to wring the last nickel out of a seller. The buyer might say, "Are there any other offers coming in?"

"I've had some calls, but seen no offers in writing," you say.

The buyer then goes for splitting the difference, saying again, "We'd be willing to pay $292,000 and not a penny more."

Now you are $5,000 apart. If you consider the verbal $295,500, you are only $3,500 apart. Go over the comps again. The range is $295,500 to $297,000. You need to get the buyer, at least, to the lower figure. First, you must explain the facts of contract life.

"That's fine, MMS, but you do understand that the seller is under no obligation whatsoever to take one penny less than the $307,000 he is asking, unless you accept this counteroffer at $297,000. You understand that as soon as you counter this price, he is under no further obligation to sell it to you at that figure, but if you do, he is!" you say.

In other words, if they take this counter, they've just bought a house. If they counter the counter, they haven't.

Some buyers will realize that the counter is market and will sign. Some won't. Some will insist on splitting the difference. At this point, you need to get them both to accept the $295,500 verbally and get one to make that price the counter. Here, try it with the buyer first.

"What you should understand, MMS, is the sellers just put their home on the market. They know the comps. There is absolutely no reason for them to accept an offer below market value on their property. An offer of $292,000, based on those comps, is below market value. You see the range is $295,500 to $297,000. Their counter to you is fair and reasonable, based on this information. They know that I have shown you these comps. Based on that, what do you think they will think if I bring them $292,000? Will they think that you are being fair as well? Will they think that you are trying to take advantage of them? Worse, could they think you are trying to "steal" their property? I have seen sellers who, thinking that a certain buyer was trying to take advantage, simply ended the negotiations, refusing to deal with that buyer further at any price. I'm not saying that these sellers will feel that way. I'm just suggesting that we don't try to find out. Why don't we try $295,500 and see what happens? If we get it at that price, you'll know you have gotten absolutely bottom dollar out of these sellers and can rest easy, knowing that they will work with you during escrow and your occupancy."

Seller Price Negotiation #2

If you can't get the buyers up, write up the counter offer at $292,000. Take it to the sellers, and explain that the buyers are frightened and cautious. You don't suggest they accept the counter, unless they want to. You don't even suggest the $295,500 counter. At this point, the buyers are being a little unreasonable, so I'd recommend a small counter to $296,500 just to keep the buyers in play and maybe even get that price, but hopefully to get the acceptable $295,500.

If you get the buyers up to $295,500, take the counter to the sellers and congratulate them. Should the sellers be reluctant to accept the counter, remind them of all the work you have already done. Remind them of the comps. Tell them that you know their verbal agreement at $295,500 is not binding, it is still their property, and they can hold out for that extra $1,000 as long as they want. The question at this point is, "MMJ, would you buy this property for $295,500 today with the hope that you could sell it in the future for just $296,500? Of course not."

If they turn down this counter, that is exactly what they would be doing.

Presenting Your Buyer's Offer on Another Agent's Listing

When you have written an offer on another agent's listing, call the agent, explain you have a signed offer, and you want to present it to the sellers as soon as possible.

It is not a good idea to call and tell this to an agent before you actually have a signed offer. First, it's a waste of his and your time. Second, it may hurt your buyer's negotiating position by alerting the listing agent's office of a potential offer coming in, causing them to get any other potential offers written quickly.

If you have a signed offer and can't reach the listing agent after a reasonable period, call the sellers, explain that you have a contract and are trying to locate their agent. Suggest that if they can't find their agent, they contact their agent's office manager or broker and see if they won't present the offer with you.

Once you have made contact, try to first sit down with the listing agent to go over your offer. Explain who the buyers are and the rationale behind your offer. It is usually extremely useful to get their support. After all, you both have the same objective. You both want to get the property sold. If you don't have a market offer, explain how you see getting to one. If you do, and the property is overpriced, go through the comps with the agent until you get price agreement, just as you would with a seller at the listing presentation. Make every attempt to be at the presentation.

Presenting Another Agent's Offer on Your Listing

When an agent calls you and says he has an offer on your listing, make sure it's written and signed. If it is, explain that you would like the agent to present his offer to the sellers as soon as possible, and you will make an appointment. First, however, you would like to go over the offer with the agent so you can both agree on a game plan.

When you meet with your sellers, explain what is happening. Tell them the other agent is going to tell them about the buyer and present the offer. After that, the sellers can respond immediately or ask the agent to leave while they go over the offer with you. Tell them that they will then have the opportunity to accept, counter, or reject the offer. Explain that they usually have the opportunity to think about the offer for a day or two, but it's usually best to respond in one way or another immediately. They must remember that emotion sells a property. Time chills emotion.

Let the other agent talk about the buyers and present the offer, unless the agent would be more comfortable with your presenting. Take notes on various aspects of the offer, questions you have, and points that need to be countered. When the agent is through, go through these points before you dismiss the agent, if your sellers choose to do this.

Attempt to get an immediate acceptance or counter. Thank the agent for the effort and review some buyer negotiations scripts that might be appropriate to any counter. Keep the sellers involved in all of this as insiders.

Negotiation Rule #2: Think "Win/Win or No Deal"

I first heard about the "Win/Win" concept at a seminar put on years ago by Stephen Covey. It made such good sense to me, I tried to put the concept to immediate use in everything I did. Covey has published this as part of his best-selling book, *The Seven Habits of Highly Effective People,* published by Simon and Schuster. If you haven't already done so, read this book. If you have, read it again!

This is practical information that works. Perhaps you have noticed that throughout this book, I have repeatedly talked about harmony: in pricing a seller's property, in qualifying a buyer, in working with other agents, and between buyer and seller.

Taking what is normally an adversarial situation, and making it harmonious is powerful stuff. Normally the agent is looking for the commission, and the seller is looking for an unreasonable price. If these two maintain this position, it is inevitable that one or the other will lose. Why?

Is this how they really feel? Don't both of them really want a fair, reasonable, market value deal they can both live with? Do people really want to hate each other after a transaction is concluded?

As a real estate agent, you cannot afford for that to happen. This is not to say that you want to be liked. There's nothing wrong with that either. Problem is, you can't care about being liked in negotiating. That kind of caring leads to Win/Lose; they win, you lose. That won't work for you long-term either.

Long-term, this is a referral-driven business. It is not your job to be nice. It's not your job to be mean and nasty, either. It is your job to be businesslike. It is your job to be professional.

Being professional essentially means that you know your business. You know your inventory. You know how things work in real estate and have the ability to educate your clients so they can maximize their investment in property. Maximizing their investment does not mean somebody else has to lose. It does not mean that you have to lose your time, your gasoline and tires, your energy, your knowledge, or one cent of a fair commission.

In fact, it means just the opposite. It means that, if you do a good job, everybody wins. It means that, if you do a good job and everybody wins, you get the referral, enthusiastically!

CONCLUSION

Plan

In chapter two, I wrote about Napoleon Hill's basic keys to success. One of these is burning desire, which I made Key #2: "Ya Gotta Wanna!"

Nothing develops burning desire like a plan. Can you imagine how it will feel, look, taste, and smell to put together an exciting plan for your life? And then go out and do it? It's incredible.

Here's something I've learned along the way. Results aren't what are exciting; it's the process of achieving those results. It's not the doing. It's the becoming.

Put together a plan that excites you, and you will be astounded by how fast things will happen. To keep success from becoming stale, you must keep planning. Ask, "How can it be perfect? What can I do today to make that happen?"

I'm not talking about the Tooth Fairy here. I'm not talking about dreaming. I'm not talking about affirming. I'm talking about action. To make things happen, you have to take action.

I'm not talking about enthusiasm here, either.

You've heard of Anthony Robbins, the best-selling author of self-development books, tapes, and seminars. His acknowledged mentor is Jim Rohn. I have been to several of Jim Rohn's seminars and have most, if not all, of his tapes. Nightingale-Conant produces tons of great self-help information on CDs and audiotapes.

About enthusiasm, Rohn says, "I mean, enthusiasm is great, but after you're through leaping about, in order to make something happen, you have to do something!"

I can just hear him saying, "... do something!"

I'm not talking about affirmations, either. People are going out and spending good money to learn how to affirm. They buy books and tapes, read, and listen to them. Then they affirm. Then they do things that will actually result in going backward. They affirm they are going to get wealthy, and then they don't show up for their next appointment. They affirm they are going to get a new car, and then they stand around the coffee room with their buddies, forgetting to make a couple of prospecting calls or see a couple of new listings. Then their life goes down the drain, and they wonder what happened.

Planning is about putting together a list of exciting goals and action steps to achieve those goals. Success is the process of taking the steps to realize those goals. Sounds simple, doesn't it? It is!

Problem is, hardly anybody does it.

People spend more time planning their vacations than they do their lives.

About these folks, Rohn says in his seminars, "Plan, plan, plan. Why, if you worked where I work, you work hard all day. You work hard, all you got time for is to come home, have a little bite to eat, watch a little TV, and go to bed. Who's got time to plan, plan, plan? This is a hard worker, a good worker, and sincere. But you can be a hard worker, a good worker, a sincere worker—and be broke, confused, and embarrassed!"

In his book, *Lead the Field,* Earl Nightingale says, "Life without a plan is like a ship without a rudder!"

People take off in their ships. Where are they going? They don't know. When are they going to get there? They don't know. Like a ship afloat at sea without a rudder, they are tossed about by the winds of chance. How many end up in a safe harbor? How many win the lottery? What is it, one in ten million? What about those who don't win the lottery? How many sailing ships without rudders are swept by the winds and seas upon the rocky shoals of life, smashed, and ruined? However, ask a captain of a major shipping vessel where he's going, and he'll have a very precise answer, "Why, we are going nonstop to Hong Kong, and we'll be there on Friday at 10:00 AM!"

And nine times out of ten, he will be.

"It's Your Movie!"

I was listening to some tapes of a seminar put on by Richard Bach, the author of *A Bridge Across Forever* and *Jonathan Livingston Seagull,* and he said the most incredible thing. He said, "Your life is your movie."

It's like going to the movies. If you don't like the movie, you can get up and leave. If you don't like your life, you can change it!

What if your life was a movie, and you were the writer, director, producer, and the star? I guess if the movie weren't as successful as you thought it would be, you'd have to blame one of those guys. And, I guess, if it was a smash hit, with lines around every movie house in every major city in the world, you'd have to blame those guys, too, wouldn't you?

Your life *is* a movie. You can write the script, direct, produce, and star in it. So, write the best script you can imagine. Get excited about it. Cast all your best friends, or don't. Cast anybody you want. Just make sure you have the budget. You want to make a $50,000,000 movie? First, you need a script, or at least an outline, a concept, a pitch. You need some details.

You need to feel a burning desire to bring your concept to life. You need to sell your concept. You need to sell the people who can help you achieve your goals on your idea, your concept. You need to talk to people. You need to take action!

Can you imagine? You have the greatest script the world will ever see, and you don't tell anybody about it? You don't share your vision? You don't do anything and everything it takes to make this cinematic wonder hit the big screen?

Is the Tooth Fairy going to get this miracle on the big screen? Can you do affirmations enough to get this up there? Will enthusiasm work? Alternatively, do you actually have to do something? Do you have to actually take some action for your movie—your life plan—to work?

A Thousand-Mile Trip Starts with One Step. Make Sure It's in the Right Direction!

All it takes is a plan and the steps required to achieve it. A Chinese proverb says that a trip of a thousand miles begins with a single step. A plan says that you are going to take a trip of a thousand miles in a certain direction, and you anticipate arriving at a certain time.

Now that you have read this book, you know how to do it. You now know the most productive and efficient ways to produce maximum results in selling real estate. The next step is to figure out exactly what you want to do using this information. Then you need to figure out the steps you need to take to do what you want to do. Then you need to actually take those steps, use those scripts, talk to those folks, follow those keys and rules. In this book, we've gone over lots of things that work when you do. We've gone over major concepts, keys, and rules, so that when you understand them and use them, you won't have to waste your time trying to reinvent the wheel.

We've gone over WDYK, FSBO, builders, open houses and other prospecting methods, techniques, and scripts that work. We've covered the listing presentation and buyer presentation games and negotiating in detail, so you don't have to work on these things for years to optimize the limited time you have to make your goal, to produce your movie, to achieve success.

The rest is up to you. Make a plan. Make the plan so exciting that you would do anything to see it happen. Then do it!

Million-Dollar Book

There's this guy. He makes a million dollars. He decides to take off a couple of years to write a book about it. He tells you everything you need to know about how to make a million dollars. All you have to do is read the book, then go out, and do what he says. Now, let me ask you. Are there books like that out there? If I were to stand in front of a thousand people today and ask how many read the book and tried to do as he instructed, how many hands would I see? Oh, I don't know, maybe one or two. I hope someday when you get asked that question, you are one of those who proudly raise your hand.

You Can Change You

You can't change the winters. You can change you. You can change your movie. You can put your ship to sea with a plan. You can have a plan so amazing, so startling, so incredible that you get goose bumps just thinking about it. You can't wait to get up in the morning to learn from another day, to watch your dreams become a reality by doing.

You can become a professional, an expert in your field. You can harmonize, educate, and insist on "Win/Win or no deal!" You can plan, you can dream, you can envision a good life, a better life, for you, your friends, and your family.

You can dream. Then make your dream come true.

Read, listen, learn, harmonize, plan, and do. In the final analysis, when it's all said and done, you are what you have thought and what you have accomplished.

If today, you are not happy with what you have accomplished, you can make up another plan. You can change.

What can you do? If you haven't read, listened, harmonized, and planned, and your life has not worked out so well so far, what can you do?

You can do the most amazing things.
Today!

ABOUT THE AUTHOR

Tom Mourning is a top-producing real estate agent and a top manager.

Dissatisfied with a corporate career, he got into real estate in 1972. With a family to support, he kept his big corporation job and sold part-time at first. However, he quickly made more money selling real estate than at his real job, so he gave up the security of a regular salary, company car, and expense account. In just a year, he was the top real estate agent in his company, Valley Realty, more than tripling his big corporation income!

The following year, he took over the worst of his company's fifteen offices. By teaching his agents the same techniques he teaches in this book, within two years, that office became the most profitable office in the company.

He achieved the same results when he transferred to another office, which in six months, surpassed his first office. Between them, the two offices accounted for 67 percent of the profits of the American Stock Exchange company he worked for.

His company eventually spun off from its holding company and was sold to Sears as a part of Coldwell Banker. Tom's second office was to become the most profitable office in the Coldwell Banker residential system. The idea of working again for another big corporation bothered Tom, so he decided to step down from management.

However, he continued to test his methods. In 1982, he did well, but in 1983 and in 1984, he was named, "America's Best, Number One Sales Associate." The commemorative plaques still hang on his office wall today.

At the same time he was winning accolades as a top real estate agent, he was also doing some home building and land development. So, after being proclaimed the nation's best sales associate two years in a row, he retired to dabble in his other projects and live the good life on San Francisco's Nob Hill. This was one of Tom's dreams come true.

Time went by, and Tom began to ask, "What in my career has been the most fun and the most self-fulfilling? Winning all the awards? Making all the money? Developing a winning team?"

The more he thought about it, the more he came to realize that he most enjoyed teaching someone to be successful in real estate. Some of his closest personal relationships have been with people he has trained. He feels a great inner satisfaction about having been a positive influence in their lives.

He determined that, for him, self-fulfillment wasn't the awards or even the money. It certainly wasn't retirement. It was the love of teaching and passing on his knowledge about becoming successful.

Why do Tom's techniques work? What sets his techniques apart? What's the total concept? What's the philosophy?

In 1990, Tom came out of retirement and took over as the manager of a small residential company, which was losing lots of money.

Within a year, he had again worked his magic. The office was full and making a substantial profit.

Tom thinks that the real estate business can and should be fun. And it's a lot easier to have fun when you know what you are doing. It's a lot more rewarding when you know that you're making the most of the time you choose to devote to the business.

Tom's training methods work. Read, listen, and practice. It will work for you.

Tom and his wife, Leslie, now live in the Puget Sound area in Washington.

"Before Tom came to my office, I was considered a successful agent. By most definitions of the word, I was. However, by adopting Tom's philosophy and techniques, I made over $90,000 in just one month."

I. Bruce Maxon

A word from Tom:

I want you to have as much fun and success as I have in the field of residential real estate.

The learning experience for most agents is trial and error. That's always the most expensive way to learn. Why reinvent the wheel?

There are proven techniques, methods, scripts, and strategies that will always work. I've included them here.

It is my purpose to counsel and guide you in learning and understanding these. Your purpose is to gain this insight so you may maximize the limited time and effort you have available, minimize hardship and heartache, have some fun, and make a lot of money!

So this is our purpose, our quest, our mission: to achieve great success as quickly and easily as possible in this fantastic business of real estate!

978-0-595-41457-
0-595-41457-5

www.ingramcontent.com/pod-product-compliance
Lightning Source LLC
Chambersburg PA
CBHW030800180526
45163CB00003B/1111